DRAMA

The Drama Classics series aims to offer the world's greatest plays in affordable paperback editions for students, actors and theatregoers. The hallmarks of the series are accessible introductions, uncluttered and uncut texts and an overall theatrical perspective.

Given that readers may be encountering a particular play for the first time, the introduction seeks to fill in the theatrical/ historical background and to outline the chief themes rather than concentrate on interpretational and textual analysis. Similarly the play-texts themselves are free of footnotes and other interpolations: instead there is an end-glossary of 'difficult' words and phrases.

The texts of the English-language plays in the series have been prepared taking full account of all existing scholarship. The foreign language plays have been translated into a modern English that is both actable and accurate: most of the translations have been professionally staged.

Under the editorship of Kenneth McLeish, the Drama Classics series is building into a first-class library of dramatic literature representing the best of world theatre.

Series editor: Kenneth McLeish

Associate editors:
Professor Trevor R. Griffiths, *School of Literary and Media Studies, University of North London*

Simon Trussler, *Reader in Drama, Goldsmiths' College, University of London*

DRAMA CLASSICS *the first hundred*

The Alchemist
All for Love
Amphitryon
Andromache
Antigone
Arden of Faversham
Bacchae
The Beaux Stratagem
The Beggar's Opera
Birds
Blood Wedding
Brand
The Broken Jug
The Changeling
The Cherry Orchard
Children of the Sun
El Cid
The Country Wife
Cyrano de Bergerac
The Dance of Death
The Devil is an Ass
Doctor Faustus
A Doll's House
The Duchess of Malfi
Edward II
Electra (Euripides)
Electra (Sophocles)
An Enemy of the People
Enrico IV
The Eunuch
Every Man in his
     Humour
Everyman
The Father
Faust
A Flea in her Ear
Frogs
Fuenteovejuna
The Game of Love
     and Chance

Ghosts
The Government
     Inspector
Hedda Gabler
The Hypochondriac
The Importance of
     Being Earnest
An Italian Straw Hat
The Jew of Malta
King Oedipus
The Learned Ladies
Life is a Dream
The Lower Depths
The Lucky Chance
Lulu
Lysistrata
The Magistrate
The Malcontent
The Man of Mode
The Marriage of
     Figaro
Mary Stuart
The Master Builder
Medea
Menaechmi
The Misanthrope
The Miser
Miss Julie
Molière
A Month in the
     Country
A New Way to Pay
     Old Debts
Oedipus at Kolonos
The Oresteia
Phaedra
Philoctetes
The Playboy of the
     Western World

The Revenger's
     Tragedy
The Rivals
The Robbers
La Ronde
The Rover
The School for
     Scandal
The Seagull
The Servant of Two
     Masters
She Stoops to Conquer
The Shoemaker's
     Holiday
Six Characters in
     Search of an
     Author
Spring's Awakening
Strife
Tartuffe
Thérèse Raquin
Three Sisters
'Tis Pity She's a
     Whore
Too Clever by Half
Ubu
Uncle Vanya
Vassa Zheleznova
Volpone
The Way of the World
The White Devil
The Wild Duck
Women Beware
     Women
Women of Troy
Woyzeck
Yerma

The publishers welcome
suggestions for further titles

DRAMA CLASSICS

DON JUAN

by

Molière

translated and introduced by
Kenneth McLeish

NICK HERN BOOKS
London

A Drama Classic

Don Juan first published in Great Britain in this translation
as a paperback original in 1997 by Nick Hern Books Limited,
14 Larden Road, London W3 7ST

Copyright in the translation from the French © 1997
Kenneth McLeish

Copyright in the introduction © 1997 Nick Hern Books Ltd

Kenneth McLeish has asserted his moral right to be identified
as the translator of this work

Typeset by Country Setting, Woodchurch, Kent TN26 3TB
Printed by Watkiss Studios Limited, Biggleswade SG18 9ST

A CIP catalogue record for this book is available from
the British Library

ISBN 1-85459-356-0

Introduction

Molière (1622-1673)

Jean-Baptiste Poquelin (later known as Molière) was baptised on
15 January 1622; his birth date is not known. His parents belonged
to the upper-middle class; his father had made a fortune in the
upholstery business and then become a courtier of King Louis
XIV, being granted royal favour and the honorary position of
Tapissier du Roi ('upholsterer royal'). Young Poquelin was given an
expensive education and studied law at the university of Orléans.
But from childhood, encouraged by his grandfather, he was
devoted to the theatre and in 1643 he announced that he was
foregoing his father's business and court position (which had been
been made hereditary); instead, he asked for his inheritance in
cash, put it into a newly-formed theatre company, the Illustre
Théâtre, became an actor and took the stage name Molière.

In the new company, Molière showed exceptional ability both
as writer and performer. The Illustre Théâtre specialised in
commedia dell' arte, the semi-improvised farce style imported from
Italy and starring such characters as Arlecchino (Harlequin) and
Colombina; Molière played Sganarelle, the leading clown. He
devised scripts for these lightweight, slapstick shows, adapting
Italian originals and inventing new plots and business. At first the
company worked in Paris, but after a few months it ran out of
money, and Molière was imprisoned for debt. When he came out
of prison he took the Illustre Théâtre on tour round the provinces,
not returning to Paris until 1658.

Back in Paris, Molière and his company found royal patronage, from the King's brother Philippe d'Orléans. Molière's first full-length Parisian play, *The Scatterbrain* (*L'Étourdi*) was put on in 1655; in 1659 he had a success with *The Pretentious Ladies* (*Les Précieuses ridicules*), and in 1662 he repeated it with *The School for Wives* (*L'École des femmes*). In 1644 the King granted him an annual salary and did him the signal honour of acting as godfather to his first child, Louis. In 1665 Molière's company was appointed the Troupe du Roi and, despite constant intrigues and arguments with rivals, retained royal favour thereafter.

In his court plays, Molière moved away from his former *commedia dell' arte* style, except for occasional slapstick scenes. Instead, he developed a new kind of comedy in which the characters' obsessions and absurdities were not two-dimensional but psychologically complex and persuasive, and which allowed him to satirise ideas and manners of the time. In the touring plays, 'satire' might consist of such things as sending up stammerers or shy lovers; in the court plays he mocks more serious topics such as manners and etiquette, religious hypocrisy (this caused most of the scandal, as he was accused of attacking true religion), the desire for social advancement, and above all fads and fashions in the arts. This is the period of his greatest and best-known plays, *Tartuffe*, *Don Juan*, *The Misanthrope*, *The Miser* (*L'Avare*) – and *The Would-be Gentleman* (*Le Bourgeois gentilhomme*) and *The Hypochondriac* (*Le Malade imaginaire*), examples of a new kind of entertainment devised with the composer Lully, 'comedy-ballets' in which spoken comedy was framed by scenes of song and dance.

In 1666, in his mid-forties, Molière fell ill with pneumonia and had to give up acting for several months. (He spent the time writing.) Although when he recovered he returned to performing, his health remained precarious, and in 1673, at the fourth performance of *The Hypochondriac*, he began coughing blood in the middle of the show and reached the end only with difficulty.

He was carried back to his house in the rue de Richelieu, and died soon afterwards. At first he was refused Christian burial – a fate common to actors, who at the time were regarded as living outside the blessing of the Church. Even when the King intervened, this decision was only reluctantly revoked, and Molière was given a hasty and unceremonious burial in St-Joseph's cemetery in the middle of the night.

Don Juan: What Happens in the Play

The action is set in Sicily: in town, in the countryside and in a seaside village. But this is not 'real' Sicily: it is as much a fantasy location as the 'Bohemia' or 'Forest of Arden' of Shakespeare's comedies. As the play begins we meet Don Juan's personal servant Sganarelle. He tells us how the Don is a man without morals or beliefs of any kind, who scorns religion and seduces every woman he sets eyes on. He has recently abducted Doña Elvira from a convent, married her and then abandoned her to come to town – a town, what's more, from which he was exiled some six months before for duelling with, and killing, a General, the father of one of his female conquests. The Don comes in, and Sganarelle tries to shame him into repentance: marriage is a holy sacrament, and the Don's behaviour is putting his soul in mortal danger. Don Juan refuses to listen. In an ironical speech, he sets out his own philosophy: that he is a connoisseur not just of a single beauty but of all beauty, that his pleasure is in the chase, in the seduction, and that a permanent relationship would stifle him. He has come to town to plan another seduction: of a young woman whose fiancé is taking her boating, that very afternoon. He has only just explained this when Doña Elvira arrives and begs him to take her back, to honour the marriage and respect God in Heaven. Don Juan refuses, and she denounces him and prophesies that he will go to Hell.

After the opening Act has set out the different strands of the situation, and in particular has revealed the close relationship between the cynical, amoral young Don and the older, more conventional and pious Sganarelle, the rest of the play develops the themes and this relationship in a series of largely unconnected scenes. Don Juan is shipwrecked on the boating expedition and is rescued by the peasant Peter – whose fiancée Charlotte he duly tries to seduce, along with her friend and rival Mathurine. In a forest, Don Juan tries to bribe a beggar to curse God, and fails. He saves a young man from highwaymen and then finds that he is Don Carlos, Doña Elvira's brother, who has been looking for him to kill him and avenge the wrong done to the family honour. To the fury of Don Carlos' elder brother Don Alonso, Carlos refuses to fight the man who has just saved his life, and he and Don Juan agree to duel at a later time. In a clearing in the forest, Don Juan and Sganarelle enter the General's lavish tomb, and Don Juan mischievously invites the General's statue to dinner. To Sganarelle's consternation, it accepts.

Back in his mansion, Don Juan flatters and bamboozles Sunday, a tradesman who has come asking for his bills to be paid. (The man's name is deliberately chosen: Don Juan, metaphorically, is mocking the Sabbath.) His father, Don Luis, arrives and begs him to repent, without success. Just as he leaves, there is a knocking at the door, and the statue arrives for dinner. It gives Don Juan a return invitation and disappears. In the last Act, Don Juan startles Sganarelle and Don Luis by claiming that he is reformed, that he has seen the light, accepted God and will henceforth live a pious and moral life. Don Luis is delighted, but as soon as he is out of the way Juan tells Sganarelle that this conversion is fake, that he intends to join the ranks of the humbugs: those who cloak themselves in a display of piety which hides the extravagant and wicked lives they really lead. Don Carlos arrives to demand satisfaction, and Don Juan demonstrates his new technique, saying that he has repented his treatment of Doña Elvira but can't fight duels or take her back because it's against God's will. Don Carlos leaves in a fury, and Juan is about to continue his nefarious new life when a thunderstorm begins, a series of visions appears, and the General's statue arrives to take him to dinner. The ground gapes, the statue leads him into the pit of Hell, and Sganarelle is left alone, indignant that this ending has satisfied everyone in the world except for him – he hasn't been paid his wages.

Don Juan

Don Juan owed its existence to the simultaneous success and scandal of *Tartuffe*. Molière's great comedy about religious hypocrisy was first performed at Versailles in May 1664 and was a hit both with audiences and with the King. But almost immediately Molière's rivals began proclaiming that – like its predecessor *The School for Wives* – it was an attack on religion itself and should be banned, and they persuaded the prestigious Society of the Holy Sacrament to use its influence and drive the play from the stage. The King and the Papal Legate supported Molière, who staged a revised and expurgated version of *Tartuffe* in November. But the scandal persisted, and soon afterwards the play was banned from public performance.

The *Tartuffe* affair left Molière professionally strengthened – Louis gave him a conspicuous sign of royal approval by appointing his actors the Troupe du Roi – but it left a hole in his schedule for 1665. His new play, *The Misanthrope*, was still unfinished, and he needed a piece urgently for performance in February. Rather than rush *The Misanthrope*, he set to work on a prose comedy, *Don Juan*, completing and rehearsing it in a matter of weeks, and it was first performed at the Palais-Royal, home of the Troupe du Roi, on 15 February 1665. Molière himself played Sganarelle, his young wife Armande took the part of Charlotte and another member of the company, La Grange (who had up till then played lovers and other juvenile leads), was given his first big chance as the Don himself.

Nowadays, we know the Don Juan story chiefly because of *Don Giovanni*, Mozart's opera written over a century after Molière's play (on which it was modelled). But in the 1660s the story was already popular. A play by the Spaniard Tirso de Molina, *The Deceiver of Seville and the Stone Dinner-guest*, had been published in 1630 and performed in Italy as well as Spain; the characters of the blaspheming seducer and the statue which comes to life had been brought to France by the Italian *commedia dell' arte* companies which performed at court for the King and his brother. Molière's play was preceded at court by two other French versions (by Villiers, 1660, and by Dorimond, 1661) and was followed in 1669 by yet another (by Rosimond). Molière could be sure that the story – and its satisfyingly religious moral, that those who defy God are spectacularly punished – would be well-known to his audience. After *Tartuffe*, he had been accused of taking dictation from the Devil; this time, there was little risk of that.

The earlier stage versions of the Don Juan story are utterly different from Molière's, and from one another. The plays by Tirso, Villiers and Dorimond are melodramatic moral parables, focusing on the Don's wickedness, his betrayal of the standards of his class and the inevitability and appropriateness of his punishment. The *commedia dell' arte* scripts (bases for improvised performances) turn both the seductions and the scenes with the statue into slapstick, about as lifelike as modern Punch and Judy, and surround Don Juan with a group of stock farce characters: Harlequin, Columbine, Pantaloon and the rest. During Molière's fifteen years in the touring company before arriving in Paris, he may himself have played, as Sganarelle, in these *commedia* versions. By the time of *Don Juan* he was no longer a sparky young comic but an established actor-manager-clown in his forties – and to resume one of his youthful roles, putting the now middle-aged Sganarelle at the centre not of knockabout farce but of 'serious' comedy, must have been an irresistible professional challenge.

The Character of Don Juan and the Meaning of the Play

In the years since Molière first played Sganarelle, it was not only as an actor but also as a playwright that he had moved far from the lightweight *commedia* style. In his court plays (for example as Arnolphe, the jealous husband of *The School for Wives*, and as Orgon, the rich fool tricked by a hypocrite in *Tartuffe*), he had written himself not cardboard-cut-out buffoons but profound characters, whose obsessions and predicaments made the spectators sympathise as well as laugh, and who were as driven and emotionally unpredictable as people in real life. This depth of characterisation was his chief addition to the Don Juan story, and it elevates the play. Don Juan is not the two-dimensional blackguard of earlier stage versions, but charming, witty, devious and (as Sganarelle says) a masterful persuader, able to coin phrases and arguments which make his listeners' hairs prickle. His way of life is not mere wickedness (as in earlier *Don Juan* plays), but a calculated choice of action – and he explains his reasons plausibly and effectively. His punishment at the hands of the statue, for all its melodramatic elements, is not the straightforward retribution given to blasphemers and sinners in 'moral' church literature of the time; the feeling we have for him as a character makes it emotionally powerful, even tragic, and instead of giving the pat religious answer to the moral dilemmas raised in the play, it raises more questions than it answers.

Like *Tartuffe* before it, *Don Juan* first triumphed, then vanished. It played to full houses until the theatre closed for Lent 1665 but was not revived after Easter and never took the stage again in

Molière's lifetime. The play, and Molière himself, were attacked as immoral, atheistic and subversive, and although *Don Juan* was never officially banned, he seems to have put it in a drawer and abandoned it. After his death, his wife asked Thomas Corneille to rewrite it in rhyming verse, and this was the version known until the mid-nineteenth century, when the true stature of the original was first recognised.

At the time of its first performances, objections to the play took the same perverse form as those made earlier against *Tartuffe*. Molière's rivals claimed that the attacks made by characters in the play on religious belief and hypocrisy were Molière's own real views and that he was mocking genuine piety. The beggar scene in Act Three caused such offence at the first performance that it was cut for the rest of the run, and exception was taken to the fact that the only character in the play to present arguments for 'true religion' was Sganarelle, on whose lips they appeared half-baked and foolish. (Molière's supporters, for their part, took the equally implausible line that there was nothing to complain of, that throughout the action Don Juan was clearly a monster, and doomed, and that his punishment was as exemplary as any devout believer could wish.)

With hindsight, one might argue that a more likely reason for displeasure might be the play's layers of irony and equivocation. Nothing is ever as straightforward as it seems: not belief in God, not codes of honour, not man-woman relationships or the ties that bind servants and their employers, not innocence or debauchery. Don Juan's arguments for individuality and self-determination are far more plausibly presented than any of the claims made for such 'good' qualities as obedience, faith and discipline. Many of the audience may have been outraged by what must have seemed yet another of Molière's assaults on the codes of polite and gentlemanly manners by which King Louis' courtiers ruled their lives. And there was another reason,

personal and political. In the last Act of the play Don Juan
announces that he has repented his past life and proposes to live
under a reformed and austere régime until the day he dies – and
then reveals (for anyone dim enough not to have noticed the
irony in his tone) that this is a charade, that he is cloaking himself
in piety in order to carry on precisely as before, and that if
anyone attacks him all the other hypocrites in Paris will fly to his
defence. By coincidence (or by what Molière's defenders later
claimed was coincidence) the Prince of Conti, a minor member of
the royal family, had made a similar public declaration some
months before: that he repented his dissipated youth and was
now embarking on a life of self-denying piety. In the 1640s Conti
had been the backer of Molière's touring troupe, but when he
turned to religion he had abandoned the theatre and all its works
and left them in the lurch; now he was a leading member of the
same Society of the Holy Sacrament which had ended *Tartuffe*'s
career in 1664. There is no firm evidence that Conti was a pious
fraud, or that he and Molière were (ever so politely) at one
another's throats, but the facts are there.

Style and Satire

In Molière's other prose plays, *The Would-Be Gentleman*, *The Miser*
and the rest – even in a play otherwise as stylised as *The
Misanthrope* – language is fast and functional. It serves the needs of
character and situation, articulating the drama without calling
attention to itself. Argan in *The Hypochondriac* arguing with the
maid Toinette, Harpagon in *The Miser* accusing the whole world
of stealing his cash, Jourdain in *The Would-Be Gentleman*
discovering with stupefaction that he has been speaking prose all
his life, all use simple words (a total vocabulary of two or three
thousand only): the jokes are in what they say rather than the way
they say it. In the verse plays, by contrast, although Molière's

lines do exactly the same unobtrusive work, identifying the characters of Arnolphe, Orgon or Chrysale as precisely as fingerprints or DNA patterns, the couplets also dazzle in their own right: the play of the syntax and the 'pull' between the rhythms of the conversation and the verse which articulates it are major pleasures of the work.

Don Juan enjoys the best of both worlds. It contains a far greater range of styles of speech than any other of the prose plays, and at times the language rises to heights of grammatical elegance rivalling anything in the great verse plays. In a play which is largely about 'performance' (Don Juan's seductions; the melodramatic grief of Doña Elvira; the speeches about 'honour' made by Don Carlos and Don Alonso; Sganarelle's attempts to 'preach' to his young master – each the assumption of a particular role to make a specific effect), Molière's own performance, as author, is one of the principal attractions.

At the simplest linguistic level is Molière's characterisation of 'ordinary' people, always one of his strongest suits as a dramatist. The various servants and the unfortunate tradesman Sunday are given straightforward, plain prose, a minimum of words to indicate both their lower social status and the purely functional roles they play. Gusman and Sunday are the most subtly sketched, their dimwittedness showing itself not only in the way they keep losing the conversational initiative – both are being conned – but in their occasional desperate, and doomed, struggles to produce fine sentiments (Gusman) or polite conversation (Sunday). The struggle between what they are and what they want to be is both funny in itself and a reflection of the psychological battle at the heart of each of the main characters. The beggar Francisco is similarly characterised in a few brief strokes: at first half servile, half truculent, then, when asked to curse God, the model of shocked and injured innocence.

In the words Molière gives to Sganarelle, he takes this same plain language and plays games with it. Sganarelle boasts that he has never had a formal education, but in everything he says he shows that all his life he has been a good, if not always understanding, listener: to sermons in church, to his master's philosophising, to upper-class conversation, to the way people in authority deal with servants and tradespeople. Given the right clothes, he plays a doctor so convincingly that people flock to him for cures and medicines. His linguistic self-confidence only fails when he meets the statue, and in his final speech, after Don Juan is dragged down to Hell before his eyes, he is reduced to the plainest of all his language, a shout of complaint more honest and unaffected than almost anything else he says in the play.

For other characters, Molière combined subtlety of linguistic characterisation with more overt satire. The peasants Peter, Charlotte and Mathurine speak dialect, quite deliberately registered as a 'comic turn' and possibly owing its origin to the farces Molière wrote on his youthful provincial tours. This is not 'real' dialect, but a kind of set-piece parody designed, like a modern comedian's lapses into 'yokel' characterisation, to be a source of humour in itself. Molière has fun with half-exact quotations from country sayings and maxims, and with the gulf between the peasants' language and that of Don Juan, who is mercilessly conning them. The very predictability of the language, the placing of the dialect humour, is part of its appeal. Characteristically, however, he rounds out this two-dimensional parody by showing us the 'truth' and humanity underlying each character. Peter, Charlotte and Mathurine are completely different people from each other, with their own preoccupations, ambitions and delusions, and their individuality is exactly conjured up in what they say. Mathurine could no more speak Charlotte's lines than Charlotte could speak Peter's.

In the same way, the aristocrats are given their equivalent of
dialect: the prose of the 'honour' code, elegant, artificial and
designed to provide a kind of impermeable shell against the
world. 'Honour' plays were a Spanish convention of the early
seventeenth century; they show what happens when the
dilemmas and emotions of real life (love, hatred, feelings of
failure) impinge on people for whom the concept of their own
honour is the main article of faith in their lives, to the point
where loss of honour is worse than death. This is the society
which Don Juan's father describes to him in this play, the society
to which Don Carlos, Don Alonso and Doña Elvira belong, and
the society which Don Juan is attacking from inside. Molière
found the style, perhaps, in Tirso's original Don Juan play
and subjected it to his usual variety of linguistic subversion.
The syntax of Don Carlos and Don Alonso is heightened,
made tortuous and strangulated, and every time Don Carlos
tries to move away from it and show 'real' human feeling he
breaks momentarily into 'ordinary' prose, only to be hauled back
into subordinate clauses either by his brother or by his
own outrage at the way Don Juan is treating him. Don Luis,
Don Juan's father, first rails against his son in true 'honour'
high style – making himself both pathetic and ridiculous in the
process – and then, when he thinks that Juan has repented,
breaks free of the 'honour' style to show true fatherly feelings
and a sympathetic character. Doña Elvira, similarly, veers
between melodramatic tears and denunciations on the one
hand, and on the other genuine alarm, motivated by 'true'
feeling, when she tries to convince Juan that he is on the brink
of eternal punishment.

Don Juan's own language is as mercurial as his character – and
the trick of it is unpredictability. Like a true confidence trickster,
he first makes himself what his victims expect – and then subtly
changes, to get what he wants from them. With servants he veers

between plain-speaking good humour and aristocratic distance. With Sunday he uses a disconcerting mixture of affability and languid affirmation of his superior status ('Take that thing away and bring a proper chair'; 'Four or five of you, fetch lights and escort Mr Sunday home'). With Don Carlos and Don Alonso he plays an amiable equal, an unflinching opponent in the honour code and eventually (to Don Carlos' baffled outrage) a pious humbug. With his father he moves from sarcasm to fake devotion; with Doña Elvira he is successively dismissive, seductive and indifferent; with the statue and spectre he is flippant; with the peasants he is a dazzling mixture of seducer and patron; with Sganarelle he keeps altering the psychological distance between them, seducing and rejecting, begging and ordering, consulting and mocking – and each of these modes has its own linguistic style. This mercurial quality, achieved entirely by small inflexions of syntax or turns of phrase, makes Don Juan one of the most varied and complex characters in all Molière's output: in prose comedy until that time, only Shakespeare had ever created characters of such richness by such simple means.

Form and Meaning

In all his plays, Molière was more interested in theme and incident than in structure. Even so, *Don Juan* is strikingly original in its handling of dramatic form. Apart from the chronological progression imposed by the statue story, there is little development either of plot or character. Rather, the play is a prismatic presentation of Don Juan himself, each scene showing one more facet of a varied but static personality. The Don is morally blocked; his life has reached an existential dead-end. He tries a dozen ways to revive himself, to interest himself in his own life, and all of them fail. When the last great upheaval comes, and he retreats into a kind of double role-playing (the seducer turned hypocrite), he talks of the change more as a rhetorical exercise than as a true decision – he seems less interested in the plan itself than in the reactions of Sganarelle and the others when he tells them of it. From that point onwards, his world gradually becomes bleaker and emptier until the statue arrives, like a *deus ex machina* in Greek tragedy, to end the action without resolving it. The part, and the play, are a sustained presentation of nihilism and inner emptiness, far ahead of their time: it is hardly surprising that *Don Juan* first achieved true recognition in post-war France, in the days of Jean-Paul Sartre and Albert Camus, when Louis Jouvet played the part at the Comédie-Française in 1947.

Sganarelle

Throughout the play, the character of Sganarelle is pivotal. He is the only person, apart from Don Juan, who is onstage for most of the action, and even when he is silent (for example in the seduction scenes or Juan's argument with Don Carlos and Don Alonso), his mere physical presence makes a powerful statement. In his way, he is to his master what the Fool is to Lear in Shakespeare's play: not so much a psychological double as a representative of those aspects of character which the Don has amputated from himself. In Act Five Don Juan says that he needs Sganarelle always with him as the one person who knows the truth about him – a statement which caused outrage among Catholic opponents of the play, as it appeared to make Sganarelle Don Juan's confessor.

Sganarelle is, however, not merely the Don's adjunct or shadow. He has a vigorous identity of his own, shown for example in the opening scene and in his Act Four dialogue with Sunday. His indignation at his master's way of life, and his simple (indeed simplistic) religious faith are counterbalanced by such scenes: in his own way, he is morally just as insecure and compromised as his employer. The question 'Why does he stay with the Don?' has a simple practical answer ('How could he survive without him?'), but it also cuts far deeper into the darkness and uncertainty which are part both of the play and of Sganarelle's own identity.

Original Staging

The Théâtre du Palais-Royal, where Molière's company first performed *Don Juan* before King and court in 1665, was built originally for Cardinal Richelieu. Richelieu bequeathed it to the King with the rest of his Paris estates, and it was used by Molière and his company from 1660 onwards. (It later became an Academy of Music, was burned down in 1763, rebuilt several times and, from 1799 onwards, was – and is – the Comédie-Française.)

Richelieu's theatre, created from an original indoor tennis-court, was a large room, long and narrow. Its floor rose in a series of shallow steps, on which chairs were placed for the audience. At each side were balconies, also with audience seats. All in all, there was room for some 600 spectators. The stage was a raised platform at one end, with an ornate flight of steps leading down to the theatre floor. Scenery was painted on boards and canvas 'flats' which could be raised and lowered on a system of ropes and pulleys. Attendants saw to the placing or removal of props and furniture, in full view of the audience. When the stage was set, the actors strode on to it, struck attitudes and began to speak. In tragedy, the poses were statuesque (often modelled on famous artworks) and the delivery was ponderous and pompous. In comedy, static dialogue was enlivened by 'business', and in some plays this was built into the script: the scenes between Don Juan, Charlotte and Mathurine, or the Sunday scene in this play are typical.

Conventions governing the audience's behaviour were also strikingly different from today's. The whole theatre, not just the stage, was brightly lit (by a huge central candelabrum whose hundreds of candles were ceremonially lit at the start of the performance, just before the arrival of the King and his principal courtiers, and equally solemnly snuffed at the end). The audience was there to be seen as well as to see. Although when the King himself was present their behaviour was fairly decorous, at other times they talked, ate, played cards, flirted and occasionally even duelled while the plays were in progress. Some stood on the theatre floor, others sat on specially-brought seats – the higher a person's social rank, the more ornate their 'chaise' – and a group of (highly vocal) amateur critics sometimes took their seats on the actual stage or the steps leading up to it. Evidence suggests that particularly well-turned speeches or passages of dialogue were applauded, and that the action stopped dead while the actors took bows for them and even sometimes repeated them.

Kenneth McLeish, 1996

Note: In the original French text, a new scene began whenever a character left the stage or a new character came on. I have kept this arrangement, but added a few clarificatory stage-directions in square brackets. The other stage-directions are all Molière's: a larger number than in any other of his plays.

For Further Reading

Although there are shelvesful of excellent academic books on
Molière, works for the general reader are few and far between.
The best 'biographies' are not non-fiction but a play, Bulgakov's
Molière, and a novel, Béatrix Dussane's *An Actor Named Molière*
(first published in English in 1937, but still vivid and particularly
fascinating for the way it recreates the theatre conditions of
Molière's touring and court life). Among academic books, the
most accessible is P.H. Nurse, *Molière and the Comic Spirit*. W.G.
Moore, *Molière, a New Criticism* (1949) is the standard academic
critical work, and Martin Turnell, *The Classical Moment* (1947) is a
combined examination of the work of Molière, Corneille and
Racine. Leo Weinstein, *The Metamorphoses of Don Juan* (1959) is an
intriguing account of all the various theatrical treatments of the
story, ranging from Tirso and the *commedia dell' arte* to Mozart's
Don Giovanni and Shaw's *Man and Superman*.

As well as books, Ariane Mnouchkine's 1986 film *Molière* is
recommended (Proserpine Editions, available on video). Some
purists object that its approach is imaginative, sometimes fanciful,
but it gives an often moving account of Molière's life and some
engrossing reconstructions of 17th-century French performances.

Molière: Key Dates

1622   Jean-Baptiste Poquelin baptised, 15 January (birthdate unknown)

1633-9   Educated at Jesuit Collège de Clermont

1642   After brief law studies, obtains his licence in Orléans

1643   Joins Illustre Théâtre company. Takes stage-name Molière

1645-58   After serving prison sentence for debt, tours provinces, writes first short plays (now lost)

1655   First full-length play, *The Scatterbrain*

1658   Company returns to Paris, under patronage of King's brother

1659   Successful production of *The Pretentious Ladies*

1661   Company moves to Théâtre du Palais-Royal

1662   Marries Armande Béjart. *The School for Wives*

1663   Awarded annual salary by the King

1664   First version of *Tartuffe* causes scandal; the play is banned

1665   *Don Juan*. Molière's company appointed Troupe du Roi

1666   *The Misanthrope; Doctor in Spite of Himself (Le Médicin malgré lui)*

DON JUAN

or, The Statue at the Feast

Characters

DON JUAN
SGANARELLE, *his servant*
DOÑA ELVIRA, *his wife*
GUSMAN, *her groom*
DON CARLOS, *her younger brother*
DON ALONSO, *her elder brother*
FRANCISCO, *a beggar*
CHARLOTTE, *a peasant* *
MATHURINE, *another* *
PETER, *another* *
STATUE *of the General*
SUNDAY, *a tradesman*
DON LUIS, *Don Juan's father*
VISION

Servants, soldiers

* In the original, a dialect part

The action takes place in Sicily.

ACT ONE

Scene: a mansion.

Scene i

SGANARELLE, GUSMAN.

SGANARELLE. Stuff Aristotle. Stuff all philosophers. Snuff's
what you need. Nothing like snuff. Everyone needs snuff. If
you don't have snuff in your life, you don't *have* a life. It clears
the passages, makes your head feel good inside, puts you right
with the world. You must have noticed. You're taking your bit
of snuff, at once you're smiling, offering it round, not waiting
to be asked, sometimes they don't even know they want some.
You want to be a really nice person, start by buying yourself
some snuff. Right. What were we talking about? Her
Ladyship. Doña Elvira. Amazed, you said. When we packed
up and left, you said. Running after us, you said. Loves His
Nibs, you said. Has to find him again. Can't live without him.
The thing is, Gusman – Guzzy – if you ask me she'd do better
to forget she ever met him. Chasing after him, chasing him
here to town? Total waste of time.

GUSMAN. But why did he do it, Sganarelle? What went wrong?
Did he give you any reason, any hint? 'My hotness has cooled.
I have no alternative. It's bigger than both of us.' That kind of
thing.

SGANARELLE. Nah. But he wouldn't, see, not to me. I know
him. I've watched him at work. I know what this is about.
I may be wrong, but . . . nah. I've seen it all before.

GUSMAN. You mean, another woman? He's abandoned that
pure, innocent lady, that flame of beauty, her Ladyship, Doña
Elvira, for another woman? How *could* he?

SGANARELLE. He's young. Hot blood. *You* know . . .

GUSMAN. But he's a *Lordship*! *They* don't –

SGANARELLE. They do.

GUSMAN. But he married her! In church!

SGANARELLE. Of course he did. But he's Don Juan. You still
don't get it, do you?

GUSMAN. Not if he's done what you say he's done. If he was
planning to dump her, why was he like he *was* with her?
Presents, notes, sighs, declarations, more notes, more sighs,
'Come to me, come to me' – till in the end he grabs her from
a convent and elopes with her. A holy convent! And after all
that he's . . . You say he's . . . No, I don't get it at all. I don't.

SGANARELLE. If you knew him as well as I do, you'd get it. It's
the way he is. I'm not saying he feels any different about Doña
Elvira. I wouldn't know. He sent me on ahead, and I haven't
seen him since he got here. But, *inter nos* (between you and
me), I'll tell you about my master. Warn you. My Don Juan is
the biggest bastard ever born. Mad. A dog, a devil, a Turk, an
atheist. Doesn't believe in Heaven, almighty God, saints,
werewolves, any of it. You can preach till you're blue in the
face, he just laughs at you, you might as well try to tell a cow,
Alexander the Great, Genghis Khan, what you believe in. So
he married your mistress. If there was no other way to get
what he wanted, he'd have married you as well, *and* her dog,

and her cat. He's always marrying: mothers, daughters, town girls, country girls, cold ones, hot ones, they're all the same to him. He doesn't need traps, spider's webs to snare them – he marries 'em! If I gave you a list of all the women he's married, it'd stretch from here to bedtime. Don't look so shocked. You've gone white. And you haven't heard the half of it. D'you *want* the gory details? Oh, he'll be sorry, God'll punish him one day. The things I've seen, the things he's made me . . . I'd rather serve the Devil himself. I wish my master was – well, I won't say it. They can turn very nasty, their Lordships, if you get the wrong side of them. He makes me sick, but I'm scared of him. I'm afraid to leave. I hate what he does, what he makes me do, but I still bite my lip and pretend he's wonderful. He's coming. You'd better go. And hey, what I've just told you, it's our secret. If he hears a word of it from you, I'll deny it, I'll say you lied.

Scene ii

DON JUAN, SGANARELLE.

DON JUAN. Who was that you were talking to? Gusman, that fellow Gusman? Works for her Ladyship?

SGANARELLE. Might have been.

DON JUAN. Was it or wasn't it?

SGANARELLE. Yes it was.

DON JUAN. When did he get here?

SGANARELLE. Last night.

DON JUAN. What does he want?

SGANARELLE. An explanation – your Lordship knows what of.

DON JUAN. Why we left?

SGANARELLE. He couldn't work it out. So he asked me.

DON JUAN. And what do *you* think?

SGANARELLE. I said I didn't know either. You hadn't told me.

DON JUAN. You must have guessed.

SGANARELLE. No offence, but I think . . . you've found
    another woman.

DON JUAN. That's what you think?

SGANARELLE. Yes.

DON JUAN. You're right. And thanks to her, it's 'Doña Elvira,
    goodbye forever'.

SGANARELLE. I knew it. Don Juan, the Mighty Hunter. Ever
    roving, ever questing. It's always the same.

DON JUAN. You're complaining?

SGANARELLE. Your Lordship?

DON JUAN. You think what I'm doing is wrong?

SGANARELLE. No, your Lordship. Whatever you want me to
    think, I think. But if you didn't think I should think what you
    wanted me to think, then I'd think . . . well . . .

DON JUAN. What? I won't be angry. Say it.

SGANARELLE. Your Lordship, what I'd think is, I'd think, to
    be blunt, that you shouldn't go on like this. Love affairs, right,
    left and centre . . . I don't think people *ought* . . .

DON JUAN. So what *ought* people to do? Shackle themselves to
the first one who catches their eye? Give up the whole world
for her, never look at another living soul? What is that, some
kind of chivalry? Wear the same suit of clothes from
adolescence onwards, cut yourself off from all other changes
and fashions in tailoring? Only fools are faithful. The Earth is
full of pretty women, and just because one of them happens to
be first, that's no reason to ignore the others. It's wrong to
have favourites. Beauty snares me, wherever I find it, chains of
roses, and I submit, I let it happen. I devote myself to them,
one at a time, exclusively – but that doesn't stop me looking at
what else is on offer. What are eyes for? I see their good points,
the gifts Nature's given them – and pay them the compliment
of appreciating them. My heart was made to love everything
that's lovable – and when a pretty face demands that heart, I
give it gladly. If I'd ten thousand hearts, I'd give them all. No
pleasure on Earth can equal the first stirrings of passion, every
single time, and the best thing about an affair is that it doesn't
last. It's a siege, a military campaign, and that's the fun of it.
You see a pretty girl, you start your manoeuvres . . . Every day
a small advance . . . She's shy, she's inexperienced, she offers
you such pretty resistance, such sweet little ploys, defences,
and you find a thousand ways – tears, declarations, sighs – to
make her learn to trust you. Gradually, gently, you make her
forget the lessons she learned at her mother's knee . . . Slowly,
patiently, you lead her just where you want her. But after that,
what's left? What have you to say to her, or she to you? The
battle's won. 'True and lasting love' is a quicksand, and if we
fall into it, we die. Instead, some other sweet little creature
happens along and the whole thing starts again. Conquering
beauty is like conquering anything else – and what general
was ever satisfied with a single triumph? I'm like Alexander
the Great: I love the whole world, I want it, and when I've
won it, I'll fall on my knees and beg new worlds to conquer.

SGANARELLE. What a speech! Did you learn all that by heart? You talk like a book.

DON JUAN. So what's *your* opinion?

SGANARELLE. I don't know . . . Even when you're wrong, you twist things to sound as if you're right. I had it all worked out, and you've made me forget it. Don't ask me today. I'll write it down, and *next* time . . .

DON JUAN. Good idea.

SGANARELLE. But your Lordship . . . you did say you wouldn't be angry. I could say what I felt. What I feel is, your Lordship . . . all your goings-on . . . I'm shocked.

DON JUAN. Excuse me: goings-on?

SGANARELLE. I didn't mean . . . I mean, *marrying* them all the time.

DON JUAN. It's fun.

SGANARELLE. Fun. Ah. I see that. Fun. I could go along with it, except . . . Your Lordship, it's a holy sacrament . . .

DON JUAN. That's my business, and God's business. Not your business.

SGANARELLE. They say we shouldn't mock religion. It's dangerous. Atheists come to a bad end, always.

DON JUAN. Tut. No sermons.

SGANARELLE. No, no, your Lordship, I didn't mean you. *You* know exactly what you're doing. If *you* don't believe, you've thought it through, you've got good reasons. But there are cheeky bastards everywhere, call themselves atheists, unbelievers, without a moment's thought. It's a fashion, they think it suits them. If I'd one of those for a master, I'd look

him in the eye and say 'You really fancy yourself, don't you,
fighting duels with God, mocking all that's holy? Who d'you
think you are, you worm, you maggot' – I'm talking to my
imaginary master – 'poking fun at what everyone else believes
in? D'you think that just because you've got a title, you wear a
curly wig, a feather in your hat and ribbons in your coat ' –
I'm still talking to the other master, not you, your Lordship –
'd'you really think that puts you above the rest of us, you can
do what you like and no one's allowed to say a word? Your
servant, for example. Listen to me. Sooner or later, all
blasphemers get what they deserve. God sees to them. A bad
life comes to a bad end. They go – '

DON JUAN. Enough!

SGANARELLE. What's the matter?

DON JUAN. Nothing's the matter. A woman's ensnared my
heart. A beauty. Chains of roses. So I've come back to town.
Nothing's the matter.

SGANARELLE. Back to *this* town. Where you killed the General
six months ago. You're not afraid?

DON JUAN. Why should I be afraid? I botched it?

SGANARELLE. No, he's dead. He won't make trouble.

DON JUAN. I was exonerated.

SGANARELLE. Not by his friends, his relatives . . .

DON JUAN. So there may be problems. Forget them. There are
also pleasures. The woman I mean is young, charming,
engaged to be married. Her fiancé brought her here. Three or
four days before they set out, I saw them together. Quite by
chance. Love-birds – I've never seen two people so engrossed
in each other. I felt . . . I don't know *what* I felt. To start with,

I was jealous. Couldn't bear the sight of them. Then, an idea.
It might be fun to come between them, to take their revolting
devotion and knock a hole in it. And it hasn't been easy, so
far. In fact, impossible. Till today. The fiancé's taking her
boating, this afternoon. My chance to get all I want. I left you
out of it, I arranged it all myself: a rowing boat, a boatman,
she'll soon be mine.

SGANARELLE. Oh, your Lordship.

DON JUAN. Yes?

SGANARELLE. Nothing. You're absolutely right. Your feelings,
your arrangements. Who could disagree?

DON JUAN. Good. Get yourself ready. You're coming with me.
I'll need weapons: a sword, a dagger . . . Now what?
Someone's coming. You bastard. You never told me *she* was
here.

SGANARELLE. Your Lordship, you never asked.

DON JUAN. Look what she's wearing! What's she thinking of?
In *town* . . . ?

Scene iii

DOÑA ELVIRA, DON JUAN, SGANARELLE.

DOÑA ELVIRA. Don Juan, I don't expect you to smile, but you
might at least *look* at me.

DON JUAN. Madame, I'm surprised, I won't hide it. I wasn't
expecting you.

DOÑA ELVIRA. Obviously not. I *thought* I'd surprise you. I was *afraid* I'd surprise you. And my fears were right. Your behaviour proves it. How could I have been so naive, so trusting? It was obvious what was going on, and still I didn't believe it. I must have been stupid, or besotted – why else refuse to believe my own eyes, my own judgement? You made it perfectly clear, a hundred times a day, what kind of man you are, and each time I refused to believe it: *I* was the reason for your coldness, *I'd* stopped you loving me. But then you left me. I couldn't pretend any longer. And the way you're behaving now proves it, proves it beyond doubt. But I still want to hear it, please, from your own lips. Don Juan, why have you abandoned me? Answer. Give me one good reason.

DON JUAN. Sganarelle will explain.

SGANARELLE. Your Lordship, what reasons do *I* know?

DOÑA ELVIRA. They're excuses, not reasons – it's irrelevant who makes them. Go on, Sganarelle. I'm listening.

DON JUAN (*beckoning* SGANARELLE). Tell her Ladyship.

SGANARELLE. But tell her what?

DOÑA ELVIRA. Come here. Why did you leave in such a hurry? There must *be* a reason.

DON JUAN. Answer her.

SGANARELLE. Your Lordship, don't *do* this to me.

DON JUAN. Answer!

SGANARELLE. Your Ladyship . . .

DOÑA ELVIRA. Well?

SGANARELLE (*to* DON JUAN). I can't.

DON JUAN. You can.

SGANARELLE. Your Ladyship, we left because of . . .
Alexander and his other worlds and all those conquerors.
That's the best I can do, your Lordship.

DOÑA ELVIRA. Don Juan, can *you* explain?

DON JUAN. Madame, I'll be honest –

DOÑA ELVIRA. You're not very good at this. A man of your
rank! Your experience! I'm amazed at you. I thought at least
you'd rise to the occasion. 'My feelings towards you have
never wavered for an instant; only death will part us; matters
of the utmost importance compelled this abrupt and
unexplained departure; reluctantly I must stay in town for a
few more days; all you have to do is leave for the country and
I'll follow as soon as it's humanly possible; I'm on fire for you;
this separation racks me like the torments of the damned.'
That's what I was expecting. Not embarrassment.

DON JUAN. Did you want me to lie, Madame? I never lie. How
could I tell you my feelings have never wavered and I'm on
fire for you, when the truth is that *you* were the reason
I abandoned you? You yourself, Madame. And it's not what
you think: it's because it would have been a sin to stay any
longer. I came to my senses, Madame; I looked into my soul;
I saw my sin. To marry you I stole you from a convent; you
broke your word to another party [*translator's note: i.e., God*];
God finds it hard to forgive such behaviour. My guilt
overwhelmed me. I was terrified of divine retribution. I saw
that, however we pretended otherwise, what we had was
adultery, not marriage, and that Heaven was bound to punish
us. I had no choice: I had to try to forget you, leave you free
to return to your former obligations. It was a duty, Madame,
a sacred trust – can you find it in your heart to stand against
it, to expect me to stay with you and get right up Heaven's
nose, to – ?

DOÑA ELVIRA. Ah! Now I understand. The kind of man you are. Too late, I understand. I've nothing left. But Heaven is watching, the Heaven you make fun of, and Heaven will punish you.

DON JUAN. Sganarelle, ooh Heaven!

SGANARELLE. Yes, your Lordship. What's Heaven to men like us? Ha! Ha!

DON JUAN. Madame –

DOÑA ELVIRA. Not another word. I won't have you laugh at me: it's feeble. I should have left long ago. I won't answer you, won't tell you what I think of the way you've treated me. I'll save my fury for revenge. You broke your word, you betrayed me, and Heaven will punish you. And if you're not afraid of Heaven, fear the fury of a woman scorned.

[*Exit.*]

SGANARELLE. Well, *that* might change him. If it only would!

DON JUAN (*after a moment's thought*). Right. Time to plan that boat-trip.

SGANARELLE. He's the master from Hell. And even worse: he's mine.

ACT TWO

Scene: the countryside, beside the sea, not far from town.

Scene i

CHARLOTTE, PETER.

CHARLOTTE. Mercy, Peter, if you hadn't happened along –

PETER. Nip and tuck it were. They'd have drownded, surely.

CHARLOTTE. 'Twas that bit of a wind this morning capsized them.

PETER. I'll tell you. How it was, I'll tell you. I was the first to see them, first to see them I was. We was down on the foreshore, Fatty Lucas and me, chucking sand at one another. Just a bit of fun. You know what Fatty's like for a bit of fun, and I'm not backwards neither. Well, there we was, having our bit of fun, and I happened to look out to sea, and what did I see? I see something bobbing in the water, coming our way, or so I thought it was. I'm looking at it, like this, see, and then suddenly it's gone, I can't see it no more. 'Hey, Fatty,' I says, 'Someone swimming, look.' 'Don't be daft,' says Fatty, 'You're seeing things, boy.' 'Not me,' I says, 'Not seeing things, seeing someone swimming.' 'Sun on water, like,' he says. 'No it's not,' I says. 'It's someone swimming. And not one of 'em neither. Two of 'em,' I says. 'Taint,' he says. I says, 'Tis'. 'Taint,' he says. I says, 'You want to bet on that, boy?'

'Sixpence then,' he says. 'Let's see your money.' Well, I know I'm not daft, I know what I see, I get my money out, four pennies and four of them fiddly little ha'pennies, and down they go. My dander was up, I'm telling you. Like when I've had a glass or two. But I know what I saw. Fatty puts his money on sand next to mine – and next thing, there, we see them, two men out there in the bay, waving to us to row out and fetch them in. First thing, I pocket that money. Then I says to Fatty, 'Come on, they want us to fetch them in.' 'Not me,' he says. 'They've had sixpence out of me already, and that's all they're getting, boy.' Well, to cut it short, I persuade him, you know how it's like, and I heave him into the boat and we row out to them. We drag them out, take them home to the fire, and they strip themselves stark naked to dry themselves. Next thing, two more turn up, they fished themselves out somehow. Next thing, Mathurine turns up, and you won't believe this, one of them starts blowing her kisses. That's how it was. I said I'd tell you how it was, and that's it told.

CHARLOTTE. And one of them's a gentleman, you said.

PETER. A gentleman yes: the boss, gold buttons, fancy trimmings. The rest were gentlemen too, even though they were his servants. Mind you, gentleman or no gentleman, if I hadn't happened along, he'd have drownded, I'm telling you.

CHARLOTTE. Don't be daft.

PETER. If I hadn't been there, he'd be playing his harp this minute.

CHARLOTTE. He's still there, now? Up your house? Stark naked, still?

PETER. Course he aint. They all got dressed again, didn't they? We stood there goggling. Never seen gentlemen like that

putting on their clothes before. The things they wear!
Watching made my head spin, leave out wearing them.
They've got hair, Lottie, hair on their heads that aint their
own hair, they stick it on top like a raggy great hank of wool.
Sleeves on their shirts they've got, if you or me tried them on,
we'd get lost in them. They don't wear britches like honest
folk, skirts they have, wide great skirts from here to Christmas.
They don't wear doublets, little waistcoats don't even reach
their belly-buttons. No neckbands, four great floppy things
hanging down in front. All frilly, lacy stuff at their wrists and
round their legs – and ribbons, ribbons everywhere, even on
their shoes, you wouldn't believe the ribbons. If I had ribbons
on *my* shoes, I'd fall handle over elbow, I'd break my neck.

CHARLOTTE. Mercy, Peter, I'll have a look at that.

PETER. Lottie. Wait, Lottie. I've something to say, like.

CHARLOTTE. Say it, then. Hurry.

PETER. It's like this. Mind, I'm speaking as I find. You're mine,
Lottie, and I'm yours, you know we promised, we've been
stepping out, we'll be married three weeks come Whitsun, but
I'm not happy.

CHARLOTTE. Not happy?

PETER. With you, like. Not happy with you.

CHARLOTTE. Not happy with me?

PETER. That's right. I'm vexed, girl, vexed.

CHARLOTTE. Why vexed?

PETER. Because you don't love me.

CHARLOTTE. Not that again.

PETER. Yes, that again.

CHARLOTTE. You do go nagging on.

PETER. Of course I do. When there's something to go nagging on about, I go nagging on about it. If there wasn't anything to go nagging on about, I wouldn't go nagging on.

CHARLOTTE. All right, then. What d'you want me to do?

PETER. You know what I want you to do. Love me.

CHARLOTTE. Who says I don't?

PETER. I can tell you don't. Whatever I do for you, you don't. Ribbons, don't I buy you ribbons every time gipsies come to village? Don't I break my neck climbing trees to fetch you nests? Don't I get Daft Davy to play his fiddle on your birthday? All that, I do, and I might as well bang my head on a wall. It's not right. When someone loves someone, that other someone ought to love the other someone back.

CHARLOTTE. I do love you.

PETER. Fine way to show it.

CHARLOTTE. How d'you want me to show it?

PETER. Like other folks do. Proper.

CHARLOTTE. How d'you mean, proper?

PETER. Like other folks do. Like Tina, she that's daft for Robin the lobster-boy. Always after him, she is. Always jumping out at him, playing tricks on him, knocking into him in passing like. The other day, there he was setting himself for sitting down, she grabs the stool and sends him handle over elbow. That's how folks show when they be in love. Not you. You're like a block of wood, not a word, not a bump, not a peep or a poke from morn till night. It's wrong, girl, what's a man to think?

CHARLOTTE. I can't be doing all that. It's not how I am.

PETER. Never mind how you are. If someone loves someone they should find some way of showing it.

CHARLOTTE. I love you all I can. If you're not satisfied, go somewhere else.

PETER. Now there you are! If you really loved me, why would you talk like that?

CHARLOTTE. Oh, why d'you pick on a body so?

PETER. That's not picking. Asking for love, that is. That's all.

CHARLOTTE. Well, don't you keep asking, and perhaps one day you'll be getting. More than you bargained for.

PETER. Oh Lottie, promise?

CHARLOTTE. Promise.

PETER. Spit in your eye and hope to die?

CHARLOTTE. You know I do. I just won't be hurried. Oh, Peter, is *that* the gentleman?

PETER. That's him.

CHARLOTTE. Now *isn't* he pretty? Aren't you glad *he* didn't drown?

PETER. Maybe so, maybe not. I'm going. A glass I need, after all I've been through . . .

Scene ii

DON JUAN, SGANARELLE, CHARLOTTE.

DON JUAN. A storm, Sganarelle. How could we have known? A sudden storm . . . it upset more than that rowing boat. But it's all right, all's not lost. That girl back there in the cottage . . . those eyes! that figure! . . . She'll help me get over it. She'll not get away. I've made the first moves already. I won't be sighing long.

SGANARELLE. Frankly, your Lordship, I don't know what to say. Heaven nearly did for us that time, and instead of going on our knees in gratitude for escaping, here we go again. They're still watching these plans and moves of yours, they'll come down on us like a – Shut up, idiot! You're raving. His Lordship knows what he's doing. Numskull.

DON JUAN *sees* CHARLOTTE.

DON JUAN. Well, well. Sganarelle, another of 'em. Where did this one come from? Isn't she . . . don't you think she's . . . ? Far tastier than that other one.

SGANARELLE. Yes, your Lordship. Here we go again.

DON JUAN. My dear child. What a delightful surprise! I mean, brute Nature . . . rocks, trees . . . and in the midst of it, a jewel such as yourself.

CHARLOTTE. Oh, sir.

DON JUAN. You're from these parts?

CHARLOTTE. Yes, sir.

DON JUAN. You live here?

CHARLOTTE. Yes, sir.

DON JUAN. And what's your name?

CHARLOTTE. Lottie, sir. Charlotte.

DON JUAN. Charming! And such eyes, such eyes.

CHARLOTTE. Please, sir, you're making me blush all over.

DON JUAN. Ah! Dear child, one should flinch from everything
but praise. Sganarelle here will back me up. Sganarelle, have
you ever seen anything so charming? Turn a little, child. What
a figure! Chin a little higher. That's right. Such radiance. Let
me look into your eyes. Oh yes, yes. Smile, little one, let me
see your teeth a moment. Ha! So full of promise, such
appetising lips. I'm overwhelmed, quite overwhelmed. I've
never met anyone so charming.

CHARLOTTE. Sir, I don't know what to say. You're making
fun of me. Are you?

DON JUAN. Gracious, no! Making fun! I speak from fullness of
heart, from the bottom of my heart. I'm in love, I declare it.

CHARLOTTE. Thank you, sir.

DON JUAN. No, no, no, no, no. It's I who thank you. Such
beauty should never go unthanked.

CHARLOTTE. Sir, I don't know what to say. I never heard talk
like this before.

DON JUAN. Sganarelle, just look at those hands!

SGANARELLE. She *could* wash them.

DON JUAN. They're ravishing, ravishing. My dear, if I might . . .
if you'll allow me . . .

[*He kisses her hands.*]

CHARLOTTE. Oh, sir, if I'd known this was going to happen
I'd have scrubbed them. Twice.

DON JUAN. And your husband, dear child? What a lucky man!

CHARLOTTE. I don't have a husband, sir. Mind, I'm walking out with Peter, you know, widow Simonetta's boy.

DON JUAN. A peasant! A goddess and a peasant! No, no, no, it's an affront to beauty. You weren't born for a village, you were born for greater things. Heaven above looked down and saw you, and sent me here, sent me expressly to stop this marriage and do justice to your charms. I love you, Charlotte, with all my heart I love you. Let me take you away from all this, let me give you the position in society you deserve. A charming picture in a charming frame. What d'you say – a trifle sudden? Ah. You see the effect of your charms, my dear. With anyone else, to fall head over heels in love like this would take six months. With you, five minutes.

CHARLOTTE. Sir, how you talk. What am I to think? I like what you say, and I'd like to believe you mean it. But they do say when a fine gentleman talks like that to a girl, all he wants is, well, you know.

DON JUAN. Not me, not me.

SGANARELLE. Not him.

CHARLOTTE. You see, sir, a girl shouldn't, she shouldn't ought. I'm just an ordinary village girl, sir, but I know what's right, and I'd die before I . . .

DON JUAN. What can you be thinking? That I'd . . . that I'm the sort of scoundrel who'd . . . ? Banish all such thoughts! I love you, Charlotte, in truth and honour. It's true! And to prove it, I'll marry you. What d'you think of that? Just name the day, and I'll do it. That's a promise, and I always keep my promises. My man here will tell you.

SGANARELLE. That's right. He'll marry you. Don't worry.

DON JUAN. Oh, Charlotte, I see you still don't know me. You think I'm like other men, and you're wrong, so wrong. The world is full of scoundrels, making eyes at pretty girls and after just one thing. But I'm not one of them. My word is my bond: trust me. You owe it to your beauty. When a woman is made as God made you, what has she to fear? How could anyone deceive her? No, no, sooner than that, I'd stab my heart like this, like this, a thousand times.

CHARLOTTE. Lord above, when you talk like that I don't know whether I believe you or not, but I know I want to.

DON JUAN. Trust me. I deserve it, I'll keep my promise. Trust me, I'm on my knees. Will you do me the honour to become my wife?

CHARLOTTE. I'll have to ask Auntie first.

DON JUAN. You see! You will! Give me your hand, Charlotte.

CHARLOTTE. You're not just talking, sir? You mean it? To talk like that, and break your word, when a girl believed you, would be a fearful thing.

DON JUAN. What am I hearing? You still don't trust me? Let me swear, let me raise my hands to Heaven and swear –

CHARLOTTE. Lord, no swearing, sir. I trust you.

DON JUAN. Prove it! Kiss me, prove it. On the lips.

CHARLOTTE. Not till we're married, sir. I'll kiss you then, as much as you want.

DON JUAN. Your hand, then. Let me kiss your hand. A thousand, thousand times, let my love rain kisses –

Scene iii

DON JUAN, SGANARELLE, PETER, CHARLOTTE.

PETER (*goes between them and jostles* DON JUAN). Mind, now. Sir's getting hot, sir could regret that.

DON JUAN (*pushing him away violently*). Who is this fellow?

PETER. Mind, sir, you don't want to go kissing her. She's my intended.

DON JUAN (*pushing again*). Mind your own business.

PETER. Don't you push me.

CHARLOTTE (*taking his arm*). Let be, Peter.

PETER. I will not let be. I will not let be.

DON JUAN. Ha!

PETER. Just because you're a Lordship, what right have you to kiss our women? Kiss your own women.

DON JUAN. What?

PETER. That's right: what.

DON JUAN *cuffs him.*

Here. Don't you hit me.

Another cuff.

Ow!

Another.

Here!

Another.

I see. I see. Save a man from drowning, and how does he thank you? He boxes ears. He boxes ears.

CHARLOTTE. Don't you get mad now, Peter.

PETER. I will if I want. And what are you after, girl, letting him smarm his way like that?

CHARLOTTE. You don't understand. You've nothing to get mad for. His Lordship's going to marry me.

PETER. You said you'd marry *me*.

CHARLOTTE. Never mind that. Don't you want me to be her Ladyship? I thought you said you loved me.

PETER. I did, and I rather see you dead than marry someone else.

CHARLOTTE. Don't upset yourself. When I'm her Ladyship, I'll see you're all right. You can come to the Big House every morning, with all our butter and all our cheese.

PETER. I'll do no such thing. Not if you paid twice over. Lord, if I'd thought he was going to talk to you like that, I'd have banged him on the head and left him in the water.

DON JUAN (*threatening*). What did you say?

PETER (*ducking behind* CHARLOTTE). I'm not afraid of you.

They start feinting round and round her.

DON JUAN. I'll see to you.

PETER. You and who'll help you?

. DON JUAN. Stand still, damn it.

PETER. Who'll make me?

DON JUAN. Haaa-ah!

SGANARELLE (*coming between them*). Your Lordship, leave him. He isn't worth it. He doesn't deserve it. (*To* PETER) Get out while you can. Don't annoy him.

PETER (*squaring up to* DON JUAN). I *want* to annoy him.

DON JUAN. You asked for this.

He swings at him. PETER *ducks, and* SGANARELLE *gets it.*

SGANARELLE (*to* PETER). Idiot!

DON JUAN. You should have stayed out of it.

PETER. Such goings on. I'm telling Auntie, see if I don't.

[*Exit.*]

DON JUAN. My dear, you've made me the happiest man on Earth. I wouldn't exchange this happiness for all the riches of India, Arabia. What delights will be ours, how we'll savour them, when once you're mine –

Scene iv

DON JUAN, SGANARELLE, CHARLOTTE, MATHURINE.

SGANARELLE. Oh-oh.

MATHURINE (*aside, to* DON JUAN). Your Lordship, what are you doing with Charlotte? Talking love with her as well?

DON JUAN (*aside, to her*). Quite the opposite. She was telling me how she longed to be my wife, and I was telling her I was engaged to you.

CHARLOTTE (*aside to him*). Your Lordship, that's Mathurine. What does she want?

DON JUAN (*aside to her*). She's jealous because I'm talking to you. She wants me to marry her. I'm telling her it's you I want.

MATHURINE. Now, Charlotte –

DON JUAN (*aside to her*). Don't waste your breath. You won't change her mind.

CHARLOTTE. Now, Mathurine –

DON JUAN (*aside to her*). It's pointless. She's determined.

MATHURINE. Is that right? You really – ?

DON JUAN (*aside to her*). You won't persuade her.

CHARLOTTE. I'd like to know –

DON JUAN (*aside to her*). She's pig-headed.

MATHURINE. You see, I –

DON JUAN (*aside to her*). Don't bother. She's crazy.

CHARLOTTE. It seems to me –

DON JUAN (*aside to her*). Leave her alone. Poor soul.

MATHURINE. I have to talk to her.

CHARLOTTE. I want to hear *why* –

MATHURINE. Why what?

DON JUAN (*aside to her*). She'll be saying I promised to marry her. She will.

CHARLOTTE. I –

DON JUAN (*aside to her*). It's obvious. She'll say I swore to make her mine.

MATHURINE. Look here, Charlotte, you can't go scrumping other people's apples.

CHARLOTTE. Look here, Mathurine, stay out of it. His Lordship and I have things to talk about.

MATHURINE. He saw me first.

CHARLOTTE. Well, he saw me after. *And* he promised to marry me.

DON JUAN (*aside to* MATHURINE). You see?

MATHURINE. Oh I'm sorry, but that was me he promised to marry.

DON JUAN (*aside to* CHARLOTTE). I told you.

CHARLOTTE. I'm really sorry, but that was me.

MATHURINE. I'm really, really sorry, but that was me.

CHARLOTTE. Ask him yourself. He'll say it was me.

MATHURINE. He'll say it was me.

CHARLOTTE. Your Lordship, did you promise to marry her?

DON JUAN (*aside to her*). You're joking.

MATHURINE. Your Lordship, did you swear to make her yours?

DON JUAN (*aside to her*). You're dreaming.

CHARLOTTE. She keeps on saying it.

DON JUAN (*aside to her*). Ignore her.

MATHURINE. She won't be told.

DON JUAN (*aside to her*). Pay no attention.

CHARLOTTE. No, no, it can't go on.

MATHURINE. It has to be settled.

CHARLOTTE. Mathurine, when his Lordship says what's going on, you'll go red as a lobster.

MATHURINE. Charlotte, when his Lordship explains, you'll go white as a cauliflower.

CHARLOTTE. Tell her, your Lordship. She's my friend, I don't want quarrelling.

MATHURINE. Explain, your Lordship. I want to hug her like a sister.

CHARLOTTE (*aside to her*). Now you'll see.

MATHURINE (*aside to her*). No, you will.

CHARLOTTE (*to* DON JUAN). Your Lordship . . .

MATHURINE (*to* DON JUAN). Speak.

DON JUAN (*feigning embarrassment, to both of them*). What d'you want me to say? You both say I promised to marry you. But each of you knows the truth, surely. You don't need me to spell it out, to repeat myself. My promised bride can simply look at the other one and laugh. She has my promise, what else does she need? More words will get us nowhere. It's time for deeds. I'll end your quarrel as soon as I marry one of you – then both of you will know. (*Aside to* MATHURINE) Let her think what she likes. (*Aside to* CHARLOTTE) Let her daydream. (*Aside to* MATHURINE) It's you I adore. (*Aside to* CHARLOTTE) It's you I long for. (*Aside to* MATHURINE) You're the only woman in the world. (*Aside to* CHARLOTTE) There's no one else but you. (*To both*) Now, if you'll excuse me, five minutes, I've something I must be doing. I won't be long.

[*Exit.*]

CHARLOTTE (*to* MATHURINE). It's me he loves.

MATHURINE. But it's me he's going to marry.

SGANARELLE. Girls, you don't know what you're doing. You don't know what he's like. For your own sakes, don't listen to him. Go home.

Enter DON JUAN. [SGANARELLE *doesn't see him.*]

DON JUAN (*aside*). Where's Sganarelle? I need him.

SGANARELLE. He's a cheat, he's after just one thing, he marries the whole world and then –

He sees DON JUAN.

That's the kind of thing they say about him, and they're liars. His Lordship doesn't marry the whole world, he isn't a cheat, he's not after just one thing. Oh look, here he is. Ask him yourselves.

DON JUAN. Ask anything.

SGANARELLE. Your Lordship, there's so much slander in the world these days, I thought I'd nip it in the bud before it starts. I was telling them the sort of rubbish people would say about you, and how they weren't to believe a word of it.

DON JUAN. Sganarelle.

SGANARELLE. Yes, his Lordship's a man of honour, that's what his Lordship is.

DON JUAN. H'm.

SGANARELLE. Whatever the others say.

Scene v

DON JUAN, SGANARELLE, CHARLOTTE, MATHURINE, SERVANT ('LA RAMÉE).

SERVANT. Your Lordship, it's not safe here.

DON JUAN. Pardon?

SERVANT. I came to warn you. Twelve horsemen are looking for you. They'll be here in a moment. I don't know how they found you. A peasant told me – they questioned him, gave him your description. Hurry! The sooner you leave, the better.

[*Exit.*]

DON JUAN (*to the women*). My dears, as I told you, there's something I must be doing. Remember what I told you, and you'll hear from me tomorrow evening.

[*He shows them out.*]

We're outnumbered. The only way is to trick them. Sganarelle, change clothes with me.

SGANARELLE. Your Lordship, you're joking. Your clothes – I could be killed.

DON JUAN. Don't argue. It's an honour. Most servants would give their eye-teeth to die for their masters.

SGANARELLE. Thanks. O Lord, if I have to die, why can't I do it as *myself*?

ACT THREE

Scene: a forest near the sea, not far from town.

Scene i

DON JUAN (*in hunting clothes*), SGANARELLE (*dressed as a doctor*).

SGANARELLE. I told you, your Lordship. These disguises'll do it. Anyone would've recognised us before. But now they won't.

DON JUAN. Not you, for certain. Where did you dig *those* up?

SGANARELLE. The pawnshop. Some old doctor left them. Cost me a fortune. Mind you, they may *make* me a fortune too. People are really respectful. As if I knew what I was doing. I've even been consulted.

DON JUAN. Who by?

SGANARELLE. Farmers, villagers. Ran after me, asked what to do about their aches and pains.

DON JUAN. You told them you weren't a doctor?

SGANARELLE. In *these* clothes? You're joking. I discussed their cases, told them what medicine to take –

DON JUAN. *What* medicine?

SGANARELLE. I don't know. I made it up as I went along. Wouldn't it be nice if it worked, and they came back to thank me?

DON JUAN. You're all the same, you doctors. 'Oh, I'm sorry, I don't know anything about curing people, but just look at my bedside manner.' Wait and see, let Nature take its course – and if things go well and the patient recovers, take all the credit.

SGANARELLE. Your Lordship's a medicinal atheist as well, then?

DON JUAN. It's a confidence trick, from start to finish.

SGANARELLE. What, even senna pods?

DON JUAN. You want me to believe in senna pods?

SGANARELLE. You're a lost soul, your Lordship. Me, I swear by syrup-of-figs.

DON JUAN. Syrup-of-figs?

SGANARELLE. Syrup-of-figs. It's a miracle. Even total atheists are converted. I saw it with my own eyes, three weeks ago.

DON JUAN. Saw what?

SGANARELLE. Some poor bastard had been at death's door for a week. They'd tried everything, were at their wits' end. Then someone suggested syrup-of-figs.

DON JUAN. And he recovered?

SGANARELLE. Snuffed it.

DON JUAN. Amazing.

SGANARELLE. That's just what I said. A week with nothing, and syrup-of-figs did the trick in five minutes. A miracle.

DON JUAN. Yes, yes.

SGANARELLE. I'm wasting my time with medicine. You're not convinced. But I can't *not* talk. It's these clothes. You don't mind, your Lordship? You said I could say what I liked, so long as there was 'no preaching'.

DON JUAN. Go on.

SGANARELLE. I want to narrow it down, what you believe in. Not Heaven, for a start.

DON JUAN. I warn you.

SGANARELLE. That's a 'no'. What about Hell?

DON JUAN. Cha.

SGANARELLE. Another 'no'. The Devil? Your Lordship . . . ?

DON JUAN. Yes. Yes.

SGANARELLE. More or less. Life everlasting?

DON JUAN. Ha!

SGANARELLE (*aside*). We're getting nowhere here. (*To him*) Your Lordship . . . Father Christmas?

DON JUAN. For God's sake!

SGANARELLE. No, be fair. Everyone believes in Father Christmas. You have to believe in something. All right, what *do* you believe in?

DON JUAN. You really want to know?

SGANARELLE. Yes, your Lordship.

DON JUAN. Sganarelle, I believe that two and two are four, and that four and four are eight.

SGANARELLE. Logical. Well expressed. So your religion's – arithmetic? Pure superstition! I blame education. Crams people's heads with fairy tales, and the more they learn the less they know. Two and two are . . . Your Lordship, I don't

know this from personal experience. Thank God, I never had
your advantages. No teacher, ever. I rely on what I see, hear,
touch, common sense, not books. I mean, for example, it's
perfectly obvious that this world we live in isn't a mushroom.
It didn't jump out of nowhere in the middle of the night.
So who *did* make everything – all these trees, rocks, the
ground, the sky? They can't have made themselves. And what
about you, your Lordship? There you are: you didn't make
yourself, your father had something to do with it, not to
mention your mother. We're like machines, your Lordship,
all our cogs and wheels fit and work exactly: nerves, bones,
veins, arteries, um, lungs, heart, liver, all the bits that go
together in order to, um . . . Say something, for Heaven's
sake. You're doing this on purpose.

DON JUAN. I was waiting for the point.

SGANARELLE. The point is that human beings are amazing,
and no professor ever explained how we got that way. I mean,
here am I with this whadyecallit in my head that lets me think
a hundred different thoughts in a moment, works my whole
body like a puppet, lets me do whatever I want. Look, I can
clap my hands, lift my arms, look up, look down, shake a leg,
turn right, turn left, turn round, turn . . .

He falls over.

DON JUAN. Your case collapses.

SGANARELLE. Very funny. I don't know why I bother. Believe
what you like. It's your immortal soul.

DON JUAN. I think we've been so busy discussing immortal
souls, we're lost. There's someone over there. Give him a
shout, and ask him where we are.

SGANARELLE. Oi! Hey! Over here! Hello!

Scene ii

DON JUAN, SGANARELLE, FRANCISCO (*the beggar*).

SGANARELLE. If you wouldn't mind: which way to town?

FRANCISCO. Down this path, gents, then right when the trees end. And look out for highwaymen.

DON JUAN. Thanks very much. Much obliged to you.

FRANCISCO. You couldn't spare a bit of change? For the love of God?

DON JUAN. You mean you *charge*?

FRANCISCO. I'm a poor man, sir, down on his luck, down here in the forest, ten years I've been here, I'll be ever so grateful, I'll pray every day for Heaven to bless you.

DON JUAN. Leave me out of it. Pray for yourself. A coat – pray for a coat.

SGANARELLE [*to* FRANCISCO]. You're wasting your time with *him*. Two and two are four – that's what *he* believes.

DON JUAN. Tell me, how do you pass your time, here with all these trees?

FRANCISCO. Praying, sir. Praying blessings on all the kind, generous people who give me a bit of change.

DON JUAN. Doing well, are you?

FRANCISCO. No, sir, I haven't hardly nothing.

DON JUAN. You're joking! You spend your time praying, and you're . . . You're joking!

FRANCISCO. Most days, your Lordship, I haven't a crust of bread to chew on.

DON JUAN. My dear man, I should find another profession, fast. Never mind. I'll give you a gold piece. Right this minute. All you have to do is – curse God.

FRANCISCO. I can't do that. It's a mortal sin.

DON JUAN. One curse, one gold piece. It's up to you.

FRANCISCO. Your Lordship!

DON JUAN. No curse, no cash.

SGANARELLE. Go on. Say it quickly, it'll hardly count.

DON JUAN. Here, feel it, all you have to do is curse.

FRANCISCO. I'd rather starve.

DON JUAN. Here, take it anyway. For the love of – humanity. Just a minute: a man on his own, three others attacking him. I can't have that!

He runs out.

Scene iii

DON JUAN, DON CARLOS, SGANARELLE.

SGANARELLE. He's mad, my master. Who asked him to stick his neck out? He'll be – No, I tell a lie. It's worked.

[*Enter* DON JUAN *and* DON CARLOS *with drawn swords.*]

DON CARLOS. They've run for it – and all thanks to you, Monsieur. If you hadn't intervened . . . How *can* I thank you?

DON JUAN. You'd have done the same, Monsieur. I do my
   duty. In any case, ruffians like those – not to intervene would
   have been practically to take their part. But tell me, how did
   you become *involved* . . . ?

DON CARLOS. I was with my brother, my servants. By pure
   chance, I became separated. Then these ruffians arrived,
   killed my horse and would have done the same for me if it
   hadn't been for *you*, Monsieur.

DON JUAN. You're going to town?

DON CARLOS. Only as far as the gates. My brother and
   I, we're banned from entering. One of those tiresome affairs
   of honour, you understand. They put such a burden on one's
   family, one's household, and they always end unfortunately –
   one either dies or is obliged to remove oneself entirely from
   the kingdom. The disadvantages of rank! You can be as
   discreet as you like, as upright, and you're still obliged, by
   your very code, to put yourself, your goods, your peace of
   mind, your life, at the mercy of every ruffian who takes it into
   his head to issue the kind of insult which no person of honour
   could overlook for an instant, at whatever risk.

DON JUAN. At least you impose an equal risk on the one who
   issues the insult. You have that satisfaction. But in your own
   case, Monsieur, if it may be told . . . ?

DON CARLOS. It can hardly be concealed much longer. And
   as soon as the world knows, what point in hiding my embarrassment? Better announce it: my fury, my plan for vengeance.
   It's this, Monsieur. The insult to our family honour concerns a
   sister, seduced, stolen from a convent. The villain in question
   is one Don Juan Tenorio, son of Don Luis Tenorio. My
   brother and I have been on his trail for some days now, and
   we heard just this morning, from some fellow or other, that he

was here, in these woods, riding, with half a dozen followers.
We followed him, but unfortunately we've lost him.

DON JUAN. Do you know the fellow, what's his name, Don
Juan?

DON CARLOS. Not myself in person. I have the description
from my brother, and of course I know what the world says.
Apparently the bounder –

DON JUAN. Excuse me, Monsieur. I'm, how shall I put this,
very close to the man you speak of, and I'll hear no word
against him.

DON CARLOS. Ah. I understand. Out of respect for yourself,
Monsieur, and for saving my life, I won't say another word.
It's the least I can do. Even so, after what the fellow did,
Monsieur, you must understand, I've no *choice* –

DON JUAN. Absolutely. In fact, I'll help you. I'm a friend of
Don Juan's, I won't deny it. But there's no excuse for him to
insult people of rank and honour, and I guarantee he'll give
satisfaction in person.

DON CARLOS. Satisfaction?

DON JUAN. Whatever your honour demands. Look no further:
I guarantee to produce him, wherever and whenever you
decide.

DON CARLOS. My honour demands no less. But as for
yourself, Monsieur, I owe you my life, I won't involve you
further.

DON JUAN. My attachment to Don Juan is such that if he's
involved in a duel, I'm involved. I answer for him as for
myself, Monsieur. He'll give satisfaction: name the place and
time.

DON CARLOS. How unfortunate! A friend of Don Juan – the man I owe my life!

Scene iv

DON ALONSO, *three* SERVANTS, DON CARLOS, DON JUAN, SGANARELLE.

DON ALONSO. Water the horses, and bring them after us. I'll go ahead on foot. Good lord! Carlos, what are you doing with our mortal enemy?

DON CARLOS. Our mortal enemy?

    DON JUAN *draws back and stands proudly, hand on sword-hilt.*

DON JUAN. Absolutely. Don Juan, at your service. I'm outnumbered, but I won't pretend I'm someone else.

DON ALONSO. You swine. Defend yourself!

DON CARLOS. Stop, brother! He saved my life. If he hadn't helped, I'd have been killed by ruffians.

DON ALONSO. Beside our revenge, that's not important. What are you saying? If our enemies do us favours, we should abandon our enmity? Compared with the harm he's done us, this service is insignificant. Your feelings of obligation, my dear Carlos, are logically absurd. Since life matters less than honour – what possible obligation can one have to a man for saving one's life, if he's already stripped one of one's honour?

DON CARLOS. Alonso, I understand the distinction, and I know a gentleman should always make it. No sense of obligation outweighs his insult. All I ask is: let me give him no more than he gave me. I owe him my life: let me pay the debt here and now. We can delay our revenge, grant him a few days more to enjoy the fruits of the kindness he did me.

DON ALONSO. Absolutely not. If we postpone our revenge, we may lose it. Heaven's given us this chance, and we may never have another. Holding back, when one's honour is mortally wounded, is out of the question. This has to be done, and if you can't bring yourself to take part in it, I suggest you stand aside and leave the sacred act to me.

DON CARLOS. Please, brother.

DON ALONSO. No more talk. He dies.

DON CARLOS. No! I won't have it. By Heaven, I'll defend him against anyone who attacks him. My life – the life he saved – will stand between him and danger. If you insist on fighting, then fight with me.

DON ALONSO. What? You take his part against me? Instead of sharing my rage against our enemy, you smile on him?

DON CARLOS. Brother, our cause is just. We can take our time, we don't need rage. We can control our passion, move not with blind fury but with dignity and reason. Alonso, I owe our enemy a favour, and I insist on paying it, now, as a priority. I won't let him keep me under obligation. Our revenge is postponed, not cancelled – and the fact that we refused to take our chance when we had it will only enhance the justice of our cause in the eyes of the world.

DON ALONSO. This is weakness, blindness! To set aside the demands of honour for nothing, for a mirage of obligation! It's unbelievable!

DON CARLOS. Hear me, brother. You're free of this. I take full responsibility, and if things go wrong, I'll make full restitution.

One day's postponement, a debt which must be paid, imposes obligations. So far as the debt to our honour is concerned, my zeal will be not doused but doubled. Don Juan, you see how scrupulous I am in paying back the favour you did me. Understand that I'll be no less scrupulous in demanding satisfaction for the wrong you've done us. I ask nothing from you now, except that you consider, at leisure, what steps you have to take. You know the scope and nature of the injury you've done us, and I leave you to judge what restitution it demands. There are peaceful ways to satisfy us, and there are ways of blood and violence. Whichever you choose, you promised to see that Don Juan gave satisfaction, you gave me your word. Keep it, please. And from this moment on, be advised: I owe no obligations more, except to my honour.

DON JUAN. What more could I ask? I gave my word, I'll keep it.

DON CARLOS. Come, brother. A brief postponement only, and the edge of our duty remains unblunted.

Scene v

DON JUAN, SGANARELLE.

DON JUAN. Hey, Sganarelle!

SGANARELLE. Your Lordship?

DON JUAN. You ran for it. They attacked me, and you ran for it.

SGANARELLE. No, your Lordship, I was just over there. You were right about running, though. These doctor's clothes are like senna pods. You'd think I was wearing medicine, not dispensing it.

DON JUAN. Is that it? Is that the best you can think of? D'you realise who that was, whose life I just saved?

SGANARELLE. No.

DON JUAN. One of Elvira's brothers.

SGANARELLE. One of – ?

DON JUAN. A nice chap. A good chap. I'm sorry we have to quarrel.

SGANARELLE. You don't. You can put it right, no problem.

DON JUAN. Yes. But I'm done with Doña Elvira. No more passion. I'm bored with her. I hate being trapped, you know that, I won't be caged, I have to follow my fancy wherever it – I've told you a million times. I belong to the whole female sex, and it's up to them to take turns and hold on as long as they can. Look: there in the trees. What's that amazing building?

SGANARELLE. You don't know?

DON JUAN. Of course I don't.

SGANARELLE. It's the tomb of that General, the one you killed.

DON JUAN. You're right. I'd no idea it was here in the – Everyone said it was amazing, not to mention the General's statue. I've always wanted to see it.

SGANARELLE. Don't go in, your Lordship.

DON JUAN. Whyever not?

SGANARELLE. Calling on someone you killed: it's not polite.

DON JUAN. Of course it is, the done thing, absolutely. He'll behave: he's a gentleman. Come on.

The tomb opens, and we see the GENERAL's *superb mausoleum and statue.*

SGANARELLE. Not bad! Look at the statues. The marble, the pillars! Not bad at all. What d'you think, your Lordship?

DON JUAN. No corpse could ask for more. He was such a *modest* man when he was alive, and this is what he planned for later! What does he *do* with it?

SGANARELLE. Well, there he is: his statue.

DON JUAN. A Roman emperor. Who does he think he is?

SGANARELLE. It's amazing. You'd think he was still alive. Look at him looking at us. I'm glad you're here, your Lordship. I wouldn't come here on my own, I'd be scared. I don't think he wants us here.

DON JUAN. After we took the trouble of calling? Of course he does. Ask him to dinner.

SGANARELLE. He won't want dinner.

DON JUAN. Ask him.

SGANARELLE. I can't talk to a statue.

DON JUAN. Do as you're told.

SGANARELLE. It's ridiculous. Sir, General, I'm terribly sorry, my master told me to . . . Sir, General, my master Don Juan wonders if you'd be kind enough to come to dinner. R.S.V.P.

The STATUE *nods.*

Hey!

DON JUAN. Now what? What's wrong with you? Say something.

SGANARELLE. The statue . . .

He nods, as the STATUE *did.*

DON JUAN. What did it do?

SGANARELLE. It . . . nodded.

DON JUAN. Idiot.

SGANARELLE. It did. Ask it yourself. See if it –

DON JUAN. You really are scared. Of a statue! Watch this. (*To the* STATUE) Don Juan Tenorio would be much obliged if his Excellency the General would come to dinner.

The STATUE *nods.*

SGANARELLE. I knew it. I'd have bet money on it. What now, your Lordship?

DON JUAN. What now? We go.

SGANARELLE. Huh! Atheists!

ACT FOUR

Scene: DON JUAN's *house.*

Scene i

DON JUAN, SGANARELLE.

DON JUAN. Never mind what it was. It could have been anything. A trick of the light, mist – we were seeing things.

SGANARELLE. No, your Lordship. It happened, don't pretend it didn't. That statue nodded its head, in broad daylight. It was Heaven, shocked by the way you carry on, sending you a sign, to make you change your ways, pull you back from the –

DON JUAN. Listen to me. If I hear another word of these dimwitted sermons, in fact if I hear another word of any kind about all that, I'll send for three strong men and a bull's-hide whip, and knock sense in you from here to Tuesday. D'you hear what I say?

SGANARELLE. Oh yes, your Lordship. Perfectly. No problem with my hearing, or your saying. That's one of your best things, the way you make things clear. I hear what you say.

DON JUAN. Fine. Tell them they can serve dinner whenever they like. (*Calling off.*) Boy, a chair!

Scene ii

DON JUAN SGANARELLE, SERVANT (LA VIOLETTE).

SERVANT. Your Lordship, there's a tradesperson outside. Mr
    Sunday. He says he'd like a word.

SGANARELLE. A tradesperson. Just what we need, a
    tradesperson at dinner-time. What's he think he's doing,
    asking for money at dinner-time? And what d'you think you're
    doing, letting him? Tell him his Lordship's out.

SERVANT. I've been telling him that for the last half hour. He
    won't listen. He's sitting there, waiting.

SGANARELLE. Fine. Let him.

DON JUAN. No, fetch him in. Hiding from creditors is not the
    way. What you do is make them think they've got something
    out of you. Send them away happy without parting with a
    penny. I'll show you.

Scene iii

DON JUAN, SUNDAY, SGANARELLE, SERVANTS.

DON JUAN (*with extreme affability*). My dear Mr Sunday, come in,
    come in. What a pleasure to see you! These fools of servants –
    I told them I was out to everyone, but that didn't include you,
    you're welcome any time.

SUNDAY. Much obliged, your Lordship.

DON JUAN (*to* SERVANT). Fancy leaving Mr Sunday to cool
    his heels. Fancy not recognising him. I'll have words with you
    later.

SUNDAY. Your Lordship, it really doesn't matter.

DON JUAN. Of course it matters! Telling Mr Sunday I'm not at home – my dear friend Sunday!

SUNDAY. Much obliged, I'm sure. Your Lordship, I –

DON JUAN. Don't just stand there. Fetch him a chair.

SUNDAY. I'm fine, your Lordship, thank you.

DON JUAN. No, I insist.

SUNDAY. I really don't mind.

DON JUAN. Take that thing away, and bring a proper chair.

SUNDAY. Your Lordship, there's really no –

DON JUAN. Don't be silly. There should be nothing between us. If *I* have a proper chair, *you* have a proper chair.

SUNDAY. Your Lordship . . .

DON JUAN. Do sit down.

SUNDAY. There's really no need, your Lordship. This won't take a moment. I –

DON JUAN. Pull it up beside me.

SUNDAY. I'm fine, your Lordship, really. I only came –

DON JUAN. Not another word, unless you sit beside me.

SUNDAY. Very well, your Lordship. Now, I –

DON JUAN. You're looking really well. Isn't he looking well?

SUNDAY. Too kind, your Lordship. I only came –

DON JUAN. You're in the pink, in fact: ruby lips, rosy complexion, big, bright eyes.

SUNDAY. If you wouldn't mind, your Lordship –

DON JUAN. And how is Mrs Sunday? Your lady wife.

SUNDAY. God be thanked, your Lordship: well.

DON JUAN. What a woman!

SUNDAY. Thanks, your Lordship. I just came to –

DON JUAN. And your little girl? Claudine? She's well as well?

SUNDAY. Yes, thank you.

DON JUAN. What a pretty child! I can't see enough of her!

SUNDAY. You're really too kind, your Lordship. I came –

DON JUAN. What about Colin, baby Colin? Still banging that darling little drum?

SUNDAY. Yes, your Lordship. I –

DON JUAN. And what's-his-name, Barker, that sweet little spaniel? Still yapping, still biting?

SUNDAY. We can't seem to train him out of it.

DON JUAN. I know what you're thinking. Why does he ask after the entire family? The entire household? The answer is, I'm interested, I care.

SUNDAY. Too kind, your Lordship. Really kind. I –

DON JUAN (*holding out his hand*). Well, there we are, Sunday. Dear old Sunday!

SUNDAY. Your servant, your Lordship.

DON JUAN. No, no, no. My *friend*.

SUNDAY. You really are too kind. Your Lordship, I –

DON JUAN. Ask for anything you want.

SUNDAY. Really, your Lordship –

DON JUAN. You've only to ask.

SUNDAY. Your Lordship, there's really no need to –

DON JUAN. What's mine is yours.

SUNDAY. Oh, well, I wouldn't say no to –

DON JUAN. *I* know: stay and have dinner.

SUNDAY. I can't, your Lordship, I have to get back . . .

DON JUAN. Of course you do.

He gets up.

Four or five of you, fetch lights and escort Mr Sunday home.

SUNDAY *gets up.* SGANARELLE *immediately moves the chairs away.*

SUNDAY. It's all right, your Lordship. I can go on my own.

DON JUAN. I won't hear of it. Dangerous times, old friend. I know what you mean to me. I know what I owe you.

SUNDAY. As to that, your Lordship –

DON JUAN. I don't mind admitting it. Glad to.

SUNDAY. Ah.

DON JUAN. I'll see you home myself.

SUNDAY. Your Lordship, I . . . I don't know what to say . . .

DON JUAN. Well, there we are.

He hugs him and kisses his cheeks.

Dear old Sunday! Remember: I'm in your debt, and if there's anything I can do for you, don't hesitate, don't hesitate!

Exit.

SGANARELLE. He really likes you.

SUNDAY. He does. He likes me so much, I never got a chance to ask for the money he owes me.

SGANARELLE. We all like you. We'd go to the stake for you. If something happened to you, if for example you were being mugged in the street, you'd soon see just what you mean to us.

SUNDAY. You are kind. But I wish you'd remind him about my money.

SGANARELLE. Don't upset yourself. He'll pay. He'll be glad to.

SUNDAY. And Sgararelle, there is that other matter, that little bill of yours –

SGANARELLE. Don't start on that.

SUNDAY. Pardon?

SGANARELLE. Are you saying I've forgotten?

SUNDAY. No, I –

SGANARELLE. There's no need to take that attitude.

SUNDAY. I just want my money.

SGANARELLE (*taking his arm*). I knew you'd be trouble.

SUNDAY. All I –

SGANARELLE (*pulling him*). Watch it!

SUNDAY. No, I meant –

SGANARELLE (*pushing him*). Just you try it.

SUNDAY. But –

SGANARELLE (*pushing him*). Huh!

SUNDAY. I –

SGANARELLE (*pushing him offstage*). You heard me. Huh!

Scene iv

DON JUAN, DON LUIS, SERVANT (LA VIOLETTE),
  SGANARELLE.

SERVANT. Your Lordship, your father's here.

DON JUAN. Brilliant! Now I *am* annoyed.

  [*Enter* DON LUIS.]

DON LUIS. I know you don't want me here. I know you wish I
  hadn't come. The truth of it is, we're the bane of each other's
  existence. You've had enough of me, I've had enough of your
  behaviour. Why on earth can't we leave God alone to do
  what's right for us? Why do we always think we know better?
  Why do we pester him – do this, grant that – with no *idea* of
  the end of it? I wanted a son, no one's ever prayed for a son as
  often or as hard as I did – and when I wear the good Lord
  down till he grants me the son I long for, instead of joy and
  comfort I get pain and torment. Day after day, I'm forced to
  make excuses to the whole world for the way you behave, the
  way you break every law his Majesty decrees for us! What
  d'you think I feel, watching your behaviour? What d'you think
  it's like, making excuses day after day, stretching his Majesty's
  patience till he forgets my long, obedient service and the
  loyalty of my friends? I can't stand any more! Look at yourself!
  To have been born so high, and to sink so low! Are you proud
  of who you are, who your family is? You're a man of rank –

and what have you ever done to live up to it? A title and a coat of arms – d'you think that's all there is to it? Our name's enough, we can do exactly as we like? You're wrong. Noble birth without a noble life is nothing! Our ancestors are there to set an example. We inherit their honour, their lustre, and we should prove ourselves worthy by following in their footsteps, by doing nothing to disgrace them. *Your* ancestors disown you. You don't reflect their glory: all it does is shine like a beacon to show the world how far you fall short of them. A gentleman gone rotten is an outrage against creation. The only coat of arms a man needs is honesty. I judge people by their behaviour, not the names they bear. If a labourer's son was honest, I'd put him above a prince who lived like you.

DON JUAN. Father, sit down and start again.

DON LUIS. I will not sit down! I'm wasting my breath, I don't expect to change you. But I came to tell you this: your behaviour has pushed your own father to the end of his love and his patience. I'll put a stop to it, oh sooner than you think – I'll forestall God's punishment, I'll make you suffer, I'll atone for ever fathering a son like you!

Exit.

Scene v

DON JUAN, SGANARELLE.

DON JUAN. Don't hesitate to die.

He sits.

Why must fathers live on? We all need our turn. Why can't they hand *over*? Why don't they *die*?

[*Enter* SGANARELLE.]

SGANARELLE. Your Lordship, you shouldn't have –

DON JUAN. Shouldn't have – ?

SGANARELLE. Your Lordship –

DON JUAN (*getting up*). I shouldn't have – ?

SGANARELLE. Let him talk to you like that. You should have
    thrown him out by the ears. I mean, your Lordship, really! A
    father telling off his son, saying he should remember who he
    is, mend his behaviour, live like an honest man – what
    rubbish! How could you bear it, a man of the world like you?
    Such tolerance – I'm amazed. If it'd been me, he'd have been
    out on his ear directly. (*Aside.*) God help me, the things I have
    to say.

DON JUAN. What's keeping my dinner?

Scene vi

DON JUAN, SGANARELLE, DOÑA ELVIRA, SERVANT
(RAGOTIN).

SERVANT. Your Lordship, there's a lady outside with a veil on.
    She'd like to talk to you.

DON JUAN. Who's this, now?

SGANARELLE. Talk to her and see.

[*Enter* DOÑA ELVIRA.]

DOÑA ELVIRA. Don Juan, don't be surprised to see me at this
  hour, and dressed like this. I had to come: there's something I
  have to tell you, without delay. I'm not angry, as I was last
  time; in fact, the Doña Elvira who reproached you so bitterly
  this morning, made furious threats of vengeance, has gone
  forever. Heaven has driven from my soul all the rapturous,
  sinful feelings I felt for you. They belonged to an earthly love,
  a wicked love; they were shameful, base, unworthy. Now all
  that burns in my heart is a flame of pure tenderness, a holy
  affection free from all mortal constraints and concerned only
  for your good, your good.

DON JUAN (to SGANARELLE). Stop snivelling.

SGANARELLE. Sorry.

DOÑA ELVIRA. It's because of this new, pure tenderness that I
  came to warn you. Heaven's warning: take note, draw back
  from the abyss. Yes, Don Juan, too well I know where your life
  is tending, and the same Heaven which pierced my heart and
  opened my eyes to the sinfulness of my own conduct now
  compels me to seek you out and tell you, on our Lord's behalf,
  that your sins have exhausted his compassion, and that his
  dread wrath is about to unleashed upon you. Only immediate
  repentance can save you; only one day, one little day, stands
  between you and the abyss. As for me, I stand free from all
  earthly ties which bound me to you. Thanks be to God, all
  passions and desires are purged from me. I intend to return to
  the convent, and I ask no more of life than to spend the rest of
  my days on my knees expiating my sins and earning, by an
  austere and strict régime, pardon for the blindness which
  plunged me into the toils of a sinful, sinful passion. Even so,
  secluded in my cloister, it will be pain unbearable to know that
  someone I once cherished is being lashed by Heaven's justice,
  and joy unbounded if I've succeeded in turning your head

from the pit of ruin which gapes open at your feet. Don Juan,
I beg you – the last kindness I'll ever ask – grant me that boon!
Be moved by my tears, and save yourself. If concern for yourself doesn't touch your heart, be moved by my prayers, and
spare me the anguish of seeing you condemned to eternal
punishment.

SGANARELLE. Poor soul!

DOÑA ELVIRA. I loved you with all my heart. Nothing in the
world was ever so dear to me. For you I broke my vows, you
were all to me – and all I ask in return is that you change your
life, stop hurtling to destruction. Save yourself – for your own
sake, for mine who loved you. Once more, on my knees, in
tears, I beg you, Don Juan – and if the tears of one you once
loved will not suffice, I beseech you, do it for the sake of
whatever it is you *do* hold dear.

SGANARELLE. How can he refuse?

DOÑA ELVIRA. That's all I have to say. I have to go.

DON JUAN. It's late, Madame. Stay here tonight. You can have
the best guest room.

DOÑA ELVIRA. Don Juan, I must go. Don't stop me.

DON JUAN. My dear lady, I really do urge you –

DOÑA ELVIRA. No! This is no time for words. Let me go,
make no more attempts to stay me. Do as I advise, that's all I
ask – and profit by it!

Scene vii

DON JUAN, SGANARELLE.

DON JUAN. D'you know, I could fall for her all over again. She *has* changed. I felt a distinct stirring. Dishevelled clothes, tender looks, tears . . . the embers were distinctly stirred.

SGANARELLE. In other words, what she said had no effect whatever.

DON JUAN. It's dinner-time.

SGANARELLE. Excellent.

DON JUAN *sits at table.*

DON JUAN. Even so, Sganarelle, we'd better follow her advice.

SGANARELLE. Oh, yes!

DON JUAN. Yes, turn over a new leaf – perhaps in another twenty or thirty years.

SGANARELLE. Ah.

DON JUAN. Don't you think so?

SGANARELLE. I – here comes dinner.

The SERVANTS *bring dishes, and he snaffles a titbit.*

DON JUAN. You've something in your mouth. What is it?

SGANARELLE. Nothing.

DON JUAN. Come here. Good lord, it's a hernia of the jaw. You: bring a scalpel. He's in agony! He may die of it! Ha! Gone! I'll teach you to play games with me.

SGANARELLE. I only wanted to see if Cook had put enough salt and pepper in. Your Lordship.

DON JUAN. Oh, sit down. Eat. I want you to do something when you've finished. (*Watching him eat.*) God, you were hungry.

SGANARELLE. I'll say so, your Lordship. I haven't had anything since breakfast. Try this, it's brilliant.

The SERVANT *takes his plate away as soon as he's filled it.*

Hey! Give me a chance! And you . . . what's wrong with your wine-arm? Pour!

While one SERVANT *pours wine, the other removes his plate again.*

DON JUAN. Who's that knocking?

SGANARELLE. For Heaven's sake! We're eating.

DON JUAN. I'll eat in peace. Don't let them in.

SGANARELLE. It's all right, I'll go.

DON JUAN. Well? Who is it?

SGANARELLE. It's the . . .

He nods his head as the STATUE *did earlier.*

DON JUAN. Bring him in. He doesn't frighten me.

SGANARELLE. Oh, Sganarelle, you're done for! Find a place to hide!

Scene viii

DON JUAN, STATUE (*which comes to sit down*), SGANARELLE.

DON JUAN. Bring another chair. Set another place. (*To* SGANARELLE) Sit down.

SGANARELLE. Your Lordship, I've lost my appetite.

DON JUAN. I said, sit down. Pour wine. We'll drink the General's health. Sganarelle, drink! Give him a glass.

SGANARELLE. Your Lordship, I'm not thirsty.

DON JUAN. Drink his health. Then entertain him. Sing that song of yours.

SGANARELLE. I've lost my voice.

DON JUAN. Nonsense. You lead, and the others'll follow.

STATUE. Don Juan, enough! Tomorrow I invite you: come and dine with me. Do you dare say yes?

DON JUAN. Of course. With just one companion: Sganarelle.

SGANARELLE. It's all right, I'm fasting tomorrow.

DON JUAN. Take a torch and show him home.

STATUE. Where Heaven shows the way, one needs no other light.

ACT FIVE

Scene: the countryside, just outside the city gates.

Scene i

DON LUIS, DON JUAN, SGANARELLE.

DON LUIS. What? Dear boy, is it possible? The good Lord has heard my prayers? Is what you tell me true? You really mean it? I can really believe it? It's amazing. You've really changed?

DON JUAN (*laying it on thick*). Yes. I've changed, put all my sins behind me. Since last night I've changed. Heaven in its mercy has transformed me; the whole world will wonder at it. God has touched my soul and opened my eyes. I was blind before, oh blind; my whole being shudders at my former sinful ways. Abominations! They haunt my mind. I'm amazed that Heaven endured them so long, didn't twenty times rain down its justice on my guilty head. I acknowledge God's loving-kindness, his mercy, and I promise to show the world how I've learned my lesson, how a human life can change. Perhaps that way I can make amends for past wrong-doing, work to win true and final absolution. To that I must dedicate my days – oh father, help me, help me, choose a spiritual guide for me who'll place my steps firmly, securely, on the road I now must tread.

DON LUIS. Oh my boy, how easy it is to restore a father's love! One word of a son's repentance blots out all memories of past offences. What you tell me now obliterates every sorrow you've caused me; I'm overwhelmed; I weep for joy; Heaven's answered my prayers, I ask for nothing more. Kiss me, son, and let your heart never waver, I beg you never waver, from this fine new course. I must go and tell your mother, share the joyful news, and thank the good Lord for the change, the wonderful change, he's inspired in you.

Scene ii

DON JUAN, SGANARELLE.

SGANARELLE. Your Lordship, I'm delighted. I can't tell you . . . I've hoped for this, I've prayed for this – and now, God be praised, my prayers are answered.

DON JUAN. You *are* a fool.

SGANARELLE. What d'you mean?

DON JUAN. You really believed it? You really believed I meant it?

SGANARELLE. You mean . . . you . . . he . . . you . . . ? Ah. What a man, what a man, what a man!

DON JUAN. I'm the same as I've always been. I haven't changed.

SGANARELLE. Not even for a miracle, a moving, speaking statue?

DON JUAN. That *was* unusual. But whatever it was, it's neither scared me nor changed me. I *said* I'd reformed, I'd mended my ways – of course I did, a ruse, a trick. I had to persuade my father; I've problems on every side, I need his help. Why am I telling *you* this? Because I need one person in the world to understand, to know the truth, who I am, why I do what I do – and you're that man.

SGANARELLE. I don't believe this. You've rejected God, and you're going to *pretend* you believe?

DON JUAN. Why not? Other people do, hundreds of them: put on pious faces and fool the world.

SGANARELLE. What a man, what a man!

DON JUAN. It's perfectly respectable. Humbug's fashionable – and what's virtue but vice grown fashionable? It's the way the world is: a parade of piety works wonders. Humbug never fails. You can't argue with it; even when people realise it's happening, they daren't expose it. Other human failings can be criticised, they're fair game for everyone. But humbug stands alone, it silences its critics, it has immunity. We humbugs are a tightknit community; if you attack one of us, you answer to us all. No one can fight us. Decent people, moral people, don't stand a chance against us. We parody their own real actions, their own behaviour, and they're so bamboozled they don't even notice. It happens all the time: young people live it up, then when they get older pretend to repent, put on piety, a cloak of respectability – and carry on exactly as before. Everyone knows what they're doing, and no one says a word against them. All they have to do is bow their heads from time to time, sigh meaningfully and cast imploring eyes to Heaven, and everyone says 'Poor souls! they're doing the best they can.' That's what I want: shelter, security, a smokescreen. I won't give up a single one of my . . . pleasures. But I'll cover my tracks, be discreet – and if anything *does* slip out, the entire community of humbugs will rush to protect me. I'll be able to do anything I like. I'll set myself up as a moral censor, condemn everyone in the world except myself. Whoever gets in my way is an enemy for life. No quarter. In the name of God's wrath, I'll torment them, accuse them of moral corruption, and set loose on them every self-appointed bigot who'll shout disapproval from the housetops without needing a word of proof. Take the world as you find it, make the most of other people's weakness – that's how to get on these days.

SGANARELLE. God in Heaven! I don't believe it. Humbug was all you needed to be a total villain. Your Lordship, I can't take any more. I have to speak out. Do what you like to me: slap me, beat me, kill me if you want to, I'm your faithful servant and I have to tell you. The last straw breaks the camel's back. The bird's on the branch, the branch is worth two in the bush, fine words butter no crumpets, who steals my purse steals cash, a switch in time saves nine, it's a long road that has no signpost, every dog has his apple and every apple has its worm. Or to put it another way: you're doomed, you're going to Hell.

DON JUAN. It's a point of view.

SGANARELLE. And if it doesn't reform you, nothing will.

Scene iii

DON JUAN, SGANARELLE, DON CARLOS.

DON CARLOS. Don Juan, I'm glad to find you. I'd rather talk to you out here than in your own home. I must know what you've decided. You know what stands between us, and the promise I made, in your own very presence, to settle it. For my part, I still insist that nothing would give me more pleasure than to resolve the whole thing without bloodshed. Is there no way I can persuade you to take the same opinion, and make a public declaration that my sister is your wife?

DON JUAN (*in his hypocrite voice*). Alas! I only wish I could. Nothing would please me more. But Heaven prevents me. The good Lord has persuaded me to change my entire way of life. I've made a vow to renounce the world, its claims, its vanities, to live in self-denial and austerity and so atone at last for the sins and irregularities I committed in the heat, the blind heat, of youth.

DON CARLOS. Don Juan, this decision doesn't conflict at all with what I ask. A man can change his life in the exemplary way you propose, and still be married.

DON JUAN. Alas! It's out of the question, and the reason is: your sister. She heard the same call, and she's gone back to the dear, dear nuns.

DON CARLOS. Unfortunately that's unacceptable. People will say it's because of what you did to her, to us. To satisfy the family honour, she must live with you.

DON JUAN. Alas! Impossible. Nothing would please me more, I assure you. So much so that I prayed just this morning, asked God how it might be managed – and I'd hardly finished asking the question when a voice answered, 'Forget her, forget his sister. She's not for you; she's not where your salvation lies.'

DON CARLOS. Don Juan, d'you really expect us to believe all this?

DON JUAN. God speaks; I hear.

DON CARLOS. You expect me to believe it?

DON JUAN. God wills it so.

DON CARLOS. You're to be allowed to abduct my sister from a convent, and then abandon her?

DON JUAN. If God so wills.

DON CARLOS. We're to accept this stain on the family honour?

DON JUAN. Take it up with God.

DON CARLOS. God, God? Is that all you can say?

DON JUAN. His will be done.

DON CARLOS. Right. Don Juan, I know what you're up to. I won't fight here, won't desecrate this spot. But as soon as it's time, I'll know where to find you.

DON JUAN. Your choice. I'm ready, my sword's ready, any time. I'm going for a walk, down that quiet little lane that leads to the convent. But I don't want to fight, I assure you. God forbid. If you happen to be there, and if you happen to challenge me – well, so be it.

DON CARLOS. Oh yes, so be it! So be it!

Scene iv

DON JUAN, SGANARELLE.

SGANARELLE. Your Lordship, now what are you playing at? This'll finish us. Can't you go back to what you were like

before? I prayed you'd see the light, once, but not any more.
You've gone too far this time. God's put up with you so far,
but he won't have *this*.

DON JUAN. Of course he will. Strict, d'you think God's strict?
Every time a human being –

SGANARELLE. Aaaah! Look, sir, look! A warning from Heaven.

DON JUAN. Not another! Can't they get it *right*?

Scene v

DON JUAN, SGANARELLE, VISION (*in the shape of a veiled woman*).

VISION. Don Juan, repent! God's mercy waits! A moment more.
Or else, too late.

SGANARELLE. Your Lordship . . .

DON JUAN. Who are you? Don't be so cheeky. I know that
voice . . .

SGANARELLE. It's a vision, your Lordship. Look how it walks.

DON JUAN. Vision, spook, Satan, show yourself!

The VISION *changes into Time, complete with scythe.*

SGANARELLE. Oh Lord! Your Lordship, look.

DON JUAN. It doesn't scare me. (*To the* VISION) Are you spirit
or flesh and blood? Stand still: we'll see.

He draws his sword and goes to strike, but the VISION *vanishes.*

SGANARELLE. Your Lordship, that proves it. Throw yourself
on God's mercy. Repent, repent.

DON JUAN. Of course I won't repent. Whatever happens. After it!

[*He makes to leave. Enter* STATUE.]

Scene vi

DON JUAN, SGANARELLE, STATUE.

STATUE. Stop! Don Juan, yesterday you said you'd come to dinner.

DON JUAN. So I did. Let's go.

STATUE. Take my hand.

DON JUAN. There.

STATUE. Don Juan, a life of unrepentant sin leads only to destruction. Those who reject God's mercy bring destruction on themselves.

DON JUAN. Oh God, what's happening? Fire, fire inside. I'm falling, I'm blazing. Aaah!

Thunder and lightning. DON JUAN *is bathed in light as the ground opens and swallows him. Flames leap up from the pit into which he falls.*

SGANARELLE. Hey! My wages! Everyone else is happy now: the God he insulted, the women he seduced, the families he shamed, the parents he mocked, the wives he stole, the husbands he cuckolded – everyone but me. After all these years, all that loyal service, is this all I get, to watch him being punished, watch them drag him down to Hell? My wages! My wages! My wages!